9/23/98

SPIRITUALITY
for the
BUSINESS PERSON

may the life force
be with you

[signature]

Other Titles by Claude Saks

Inescapable Journey
A Spiritual Adventure
1995

Strong Brew
One Man's Prelude to Change
1996

SPIRITUALITY
for the
BUSINESS PERSON
INNER PRACTICES FOR SUCCESS

CLAUDE SAKS

ℋEARTSFIRE ℬOOKS

Library of Congress Cataloging-in-Publication Data

Saks, Claude.
    SPIRITUALITY FOR THE BUSINESS PERSON: Inner practices for success/Claude Saks.
        p. cm.
    Includes bibliographical references.
    ISBN 1-889797-20-0 (hardcover) : $14.95

    1. Businesspeople—Religious life.   I. Title
    BL625.9.B87S24 1998   98–12439
    291.4'4--dc21   CIP

Cover design by Cisneros Design
Book design and text composition by John Cole GRAPHIC DESIGNER
Printed in Canada
Text is set in Adobe Minion

First edition 1998
10 9 8 7 6 5 4 3 2 1

Heartsfire Books: 800.988.5170
500 N. Guadalupe Street, Suite G465
Santa Fe, New Mexico 87501 USA

Email: heartsfirebooks@heartsfirebooks.com

Visit us at http://www.heartsfirebooks.com

If you are unable to order this book from your local bookseller, you may order directly from the publisher. Quantity discounts for organizations are available.

CONTENTS

ACKNOWLEDGMENTS

I would like to thank all my business relations, whether they were bosses, employees, partners, or co-workers, for the excitement and energy they shared with me. For it was here in the arena of commerce that I got in touch with the challenges and joys that so well reflected the life force.

Most importantly, I give thanks to my spiritual teachers and guides on all planes of existence who have shown me the way to fulfillment and peace, especially Master Chia, Khempo Gyaltsen, M. Morgan, and Yokar.

I would like to thank my wife, Bette, who has been my partner in my journey and a great help in reviewing and preparing this book. I acknowledge with thanks Victor Rugg for the picture of me that appears on the back flap, Juan Li for his helpful illustrations, my editors, Tom Grady and Lisa Zuniga, as well as those who have walked along the same path as mine for however brief a period.

In the greatest confusion, there is still an open channel to the soul. It may be difficult to find because by mid-life it is overgrown, and some of the wildest thickets that surround it grow out of what we describe as our education. But the channel is always there, and it is our business to keep it open, to have access to the deepest part of ourselves.

—Saul Bellow

I do not live in a cave, nor do I have a shaved head. I have, however, been a student of great spiritual masters, and I have traveled to many corners of the earth in search of truth, myself, enlightenment, and an understanding of how to be a more conscious person in business and in life. Business people have an urge—if not a passion—to succeed. In my case, I had a rage to succeed and I wound up with a heart attack at age thirty-nine.

The doctors told me that my left descending artery was 90 percent blocked and that I would need bypass surgery immediately. I smiled at the surgeon and said, "Let's get on with it. I have massive positions on, both in coffee and currencies, and I need to get back to work." At the time, my company was rated seventeenth out of the top fifty coffee importers in the United States. After bypass surgery, I eventually realized that my rage to succeed was not in accordance with the life force—what I have come to understand as the current of Universal Knowledge —and therefore, I had been stopped in my tracks. I became more aware of my relationships with family, friends, partners, employees, and everyone and everything around me. This sudden stop planted the seed of spirituality in me, and I learned to incorporate various methods or "tools" of spirit into my business life. These pursuits didn't interfere with my life in business; in fact, within three years, my company grew to be the largest coffee importing firm in the United States.

A few simple definitions before we go on:

Consciousness: Our greater awareness as we relate to the life force and its communication from Universal Knowledge.

Full Intent: Aligning the complete self—physically, emotionally, mentally, and spiritually—in order to facilitate business decisions.

Spirituality: The act of connecting to a source of knowledge that is greater than our computer-like brain. You may call it God/Goddess, the higher self, a spirit guide, an angel, or anything else that suits you; I call it Universal Knowledge.

Universal Knowledge: Intelligence and information that is greater than and beyond our normal perceptions.

Life Force: The movement or current of Universal Knowledge throughout existence.

Meditation: A combination of active energy movement and the development of quiet, inner knowing.

Most of us go through life believing that we usually function at a reasonably alert level of consciousness, yet when we look back to our earlier years, we realize that had we utilized greater consciousness or clearer awareness, we might have made different decisions. Indeed, life would be changed completely if we could relive our decisions with our present consciousness. When I was first enjoying success in business, making a lot of money, driving fast cars, and dining in the finest international restaurants, no one could have approached me with the idea that my consciousness could have used some expansion, some deepening, some greater connection and clarity. It was only when spirituality came into my life that my consciousness expanded, and with it my success and satisfaction in business. I came to understand that, with greater consciousness, my growth and success would have accelerated, and what I accomplished in fifty years might have been done in twenty-five.

After my heart attack, I started to pursue various paths of meditation, mainly to lower my blood pressure and calm myself down. Although it disclosed itself subtly, an important business benefit also manifested through these meditations. As my health improved, my partner and I decided we wanted to expand our business and compete against the big dogs. We hired an expert to help us expand into Central American coffees. And while my forté had always been to negotiate deals mainly in Africa and the Far East, when an opportunity arose to make a government coffee connection in Mexico, I decided to handle it personally (even though I did not speak Spanish and knew little about Mexican coffees). Although I could not justify it on an intellectual basis, I came to this decision in a morning meditation. You might say it was a gut decision. The negotiations went well, and within a year we were the largest Mexican importer. Only later did I understand that our company's new Central American expert had technical knowledge and ability to negotiate with shippers and planters but was inexperienced in dealing with government officials. Meditation had brought me clarity of action and my mind justified the decision afterward.

Various spiritual traditions tell us that we are all connected. What does this mean and how does that apply to our business involvements? We are informed by the scientific community that when monkeys on one side of the globe learn something new, monkeys on the other side soon exhibit the same behavior. We are continually amazed at how new ideas and discoveries seem to occur at the same time in different research centers or countries. It would appear that Universal Knowledge carries this information through the life force in all time and space. I found that after a few years of meditation I was receiving information beyond my experience or perception. When we are in deep meditation we feel the connection to Universal Knowledge. I hope to guide you to this awareness for yourself. I am a certified meditation teacher, and over the last ten years I have explored how to best explain and transmit spiritual concepts and practices. This book is a summation in the simplest form I could conceive of to introduce to you the tools and practices that will connect you more consciously to the life force and thereby enhance your business decisions and actions. When we are fully connected to greater consciousness we have greater clarity in our business actions.

I will show you how to tap into this knowledge. To

keep our bodies fit, we need to include regular exercise. Similarly, to tap into Universal Knowledge and expand our consciousness, we need to practice and exercise our spiritual channels. You will have to work with these practices to obtain positive results in decision-making, problem-solving, and other aspects of your business life. I believe that once we connect to Universal Knowledge we cannot help but behave for the greater good of our customers, ourselves, and the planet. Spirituality is not about morality or ethics, although the outcome may address these principles, it is about reconnecting to primary perception; the molecular connection to Universal Knowledge. This full connection to Universal Knowledge will automatically guide you to walk impeccably in your life and business. By impeccably I mean behaving flawlessly for the best outcome.

One caveat, however, is that the information in this book is not actually linear, although it has been presented as such for easier access. Each piece of information you acquire can then be used to go back and enhance the previous practice you have learned. The more you can assimilate the individual teachings, the greater your understanding of the whole and the more effective you may become as a business person.

I have thirty-five years of experience in various businesses and professions ranging from engineering to running the largest coffee-importing firm in the United States, to organizing and running a publishing company while writing this, my third book. I have pursued various spiritual paths and practices for more than twenty years, and it is this inner work that has brought me the greatest success in my business undertakings. What at first appeared to be an oxymoron—business and spirituality—turned out to be a sacred dance of self. It is through this dance that I found my true self and achieved greater consciousness.

This book does not intend to get you on any particular path, but rather to give you the basic tools for understanding the deeper realities underlying the opportunities, choices, and problems encountered in the business world. You may have no spiritual or religious background, you may follow a mainstream religion, or you may engage in an alternative practice. No matter. The tools and discussion in this book can be used by people of any walk of life or spiritual inclination. You do not need to wear special clothing or attend services. You are in charge, so allow yourself to take responsibility for the practices and adapt them to your own needs and priorities. Consciousness and a true, spiritual impeccability have nothing to do with an espoused path but rather with the individual's urge to be conscious, the urge to engage the life force and truly connect with Universal Knowledge.

Because I am a Westerner living in the United States, a land of democracy and capitalism, I believe that our spiritual quest must incorporate and be understood in simple English and within the parameters of everyday living situations. The more I have studied and searched at the higher levels of mysticism, the more I have come to understand that in spirit, everything comes together; we are all seeking and talking about the same thing. A few years ago there was an ecumenical meeting of high-ranking religious leaders that included Christians and

Jews, Hindus and Moslems, as well as the Dalai Lama. At the beginning of his talk, His Holiness stated that Buddhists do not hold a view, or idea, of God; this perspective did not seem to raise doubts in the other participants about the sincerity of the Buddhist quest for the Divine. This diversity of views is natural. Universal Knowledge is a consciousness greater than all the intelligence of the universe; it is more powerful than a billion suns and more gentle than the down of a feather brushing against your skin.

I have no intention of trying to figure out Universal Knowledge. Rather, my intent is to work with and more deeply connect to what I have come to understand as the life force that emanates from Universal Knowledge, in order to assist you in heightening your consciousness and increasing your effectiveness in the business world.

Spiritual practices, or consciousness work, brought me clarity in business decisions and interactions. These practices have redefined for me the success in my present business, which still involves profit and the bottom line, but not at the expense of joy and all that life has to offer. The purpose of the tools discussed and presented in this book is to help you:

- Reach a relaxed centeredness.
- Heighten your awareness in business situations.
- Reach full intent and clarity in your business.
- Heighten your consciousness for better business decisions.
- Become more connected to Universal Knowledge in order to trust your decisions and actions in business.
- Become more connected to the life force in order to function in business with the ebb and flow of developments.
- Deepen your connection with and knowing of the above, through spiritual practices.

I discovered that as my awareness, consciousness, and connection to Universal Knowledge and the life force expanded, I behaved with full intent for the highest good no matter what the outcome. I trusted in the spiritual process and in turn was supported through difficult situations.

For example, when I was in the coffee business, we had a problem in the African country of Uganda, whose dictator was Idi Amin. Idi Amin's regime was repressive, with no consideration for human rights, while Uganda labored under political and economic turmoil. My company was the largest importer of coffees from Africa as a whole and specifically from Uganda. Although we had been publicly criticized in the United States press for our extensive purchases in Uganda, what we could not state then was that we were supporters of the rebel faction. The head of the Uganda Coffee Marketing Board, Musoke, was a good friend and a rebel sympathizer, his village being in rebel territory and already beyond the government's repressive control. Idi Amin decided he wanted his own political crony as head of the marketing board since coffee represented more than 90 percent of Uganda's foreign exchange. Our friend Musoke was accused of giving us an unduly favorable contract and consequently thrown in jail, a sure death sentence. What to do?

I intensified my meditation practices and felt connected to all levels of Universal Knowledge. When danger lurks, our entire physical system goes into heightened awareness, and meditation adds sensitivity to the total flow of the life force. Through meditation, I received clear impressions that we needed to stand by Musoke, not only for humanitarian reasons but to clear our name throughout the coffee trade. These impressions remained jumbled and unclear for several days until, during a meditation, I discerned a courtroom scene. I did not understand what Universal Knowledge was communicating, but I had to trust the perceptions and information I was receiving through these spiritual practices. I called for a meeting of all of our traders and suggested we hire a lawyer to defend Musoke. Everyone pointed out that no Ugandan lawyer was about to oppose Idi Amin, if he valued his career or his skin. This incident had been picked up by both the Kenyan and British press, and the name of our company once again had been maligned. I decided to use the publicity to our advantage by announcing openly that we were hiring a Kenyan lawyer to fly to Kampala,

Uganda, to defend Musoke and our good name. Both Kenya and Uganda share the same British laws so, after a search, we found a young Kenyan who was prepared to take our case, provided we flew him into Kampala in the morning and back to Nairobi again in the evening. We publicized the whole affair in the press, both as a protection for the lawyer's safety in Uganda as well as to put pressure on the Idi Amin regime while bringing the case to light. In accordance with the contract, we also went to arbitration in New York City. Based on the evidence submitted, the ruling was unanimously in our favor. Since the charges were completely trumped up, the Uganda court in ten days' time released Musoke into house arrest in his own village, out of the regime's police control, not dismissing the case but postponing it.

Although temporarily free, Musoke would never get a high-level job again, and if he traveled out of his village he might disappear forever, thereby closing the case. After deep meditation, I was struck by a feeling of responsibility for this bright man and a desire to assure safety for him and his family, which appeared to be in extreme danger. This meditation made clear that the appropriate path was to act through trusted connections in Kenya to move this family toward security in Nairobi. In a week, Musoke and his family reached this destination.

Although dramatic in nature, this story demonstrates the clarity of purpose and action possible through meditation. As we proceed together with these practices, I will relate other business stories to illustrate the specific use of spiritual concepts.

Picture yourself trudging through a jungle in search of a river destination (the life force of Universal Knowledge), and imagine using a machete to clear a path. Just because the machete is solid and sharp does not guarantee how long it will take you to reach the river, nor what obstacles or detours you might encounter. Similarly, I can only give you the tools and explain to you how to use these spiritual implements for your business activities. You must be the one who does the practice and you will decide when, where, and how to use the tools.

CHAPTER 1

HEIGHTENED AWARENESS
Allow!

We have all heard the expression *gut reaction*. It reflects a person's heightened awareness of the body's reaction to a situation, what certain spiritual teachers refer to as the "belly brain." Our physical body is the densest part of who we are, yet reflects or communicates to us the subtler parts of ourselves and is connected to Universal Knowledge at all times. We just need to develop that awareness.

Before approaching the first meditation practice, try a simple breathing exercise that will make you more aware of your breath, something that is with you all the time, day and night. When a stressful business situation arises, most of us have a tendency to hold our breath or take shallow breaths during the crisis. Doing so only increases the tension and makes us less attuned to all the dynamics of the situation. The following brief exercise will help start the heightened-awareness process. While you read, or as you put this book down for a moment, become aware of where you are breathing— whether in your chest, in your abdomen, in both, or throughout your whole body. Some spiritual practices involve structuring or formally monitoring your breath. This one does not. Just breathe naturally, easily, in a relaxed way. Be aware where you breathe and be aware of your natural rhythm, then breathe deeply, feeling your breath expand down into your belly. You can watch your belly move and even sense, or imagine, your diaphragm between your chest cavity and the lower torso expanding down as you breathe. Then exhale fully, letting *all* your breath go. Sense how relaxed you feel just breathing. Now become aware of your chest cavity and your breath reaching all the way up to where your clavicle runs across your upper chest. You are becoming more aware of your body, yourself, and your connection to oxygen, which supports your life. Breathe in a relaxed manner and become aware of the rhythm of breath as it permeates your whole body. You might even become aware of your heartbeat as your breathing stabilizes into a rhythm. Enjoy this relaxed breathing and be aware of yourself. The practices in this book do not require specific breathing patterns; just allow your breath to be naturally whatever it may be for you. This simple breathing exercise allows you to reconnect to yourself even in the midst of a hectic business meeting. Focus ten seconds on your breath and relax.

The practice that follows will further heighten your awareness; it can be accomplished in three minutes or thirty minutes, depending on your schedule. The practice, called "the smile down," can be used as a brief self-connection or meditation by the busy person in the morning, at an appropriate moment during the day, or in the evening to calm down and become centered after an involved workday. I remember the first time I did the smile down. I felt silly doing what I perceived to be a waste of time with questionable benefits. I remained fidgety until I let go of my mind-analysis and accepted doing the practice for its own sake.

The Smile Down Outline

Read through and familiarize yourself with this practice so that it can be followed comfortably as outlined.

1. Sit in a comfortable chair with your lower legs perpendicular to your thighs—that is, thighs parallel to the floor. If you are tall, I recommend a cushion to raise the level of the seat and avoid lower back pain. Both feet should be on the floor and the vertebrae in your back should be straight as a string of pearls hanging by an invisible thread through the crown of your head. Sitting away from the back of the chair usually helps you attain better posture. Keep your shoulders relaxed and your chin slightly tucked in.

2. Place your tongue at the roof of the mouth—anywhere it feels comfortable. Our bodies have an energy channel up our spine and down the front of the torso. When we develop tension or emotional constriction, the energy flow along these channels will manifest phys-

ically in some form. My intent here is to help you keep your energy flow as smooth and open as possible. Your tongue acts as a switch between the back and front energy channels.

3. Place your left hand, palm up, in your lap and clasp your right hand over it, palm down. Keep your hands relaxed in this position.

4. The smile down meditation consists of smiling to yourself, particularly in the eyes because they affect the parasympathetic nervous system. When you meet somebody whose entire face smiles at you, particularly the eyes, you feel relaxed. Feel yourself smile in your eyes; this will help your body relax and feel content.

5. Close your eyes and, in front of your eyes, picture a light golden or white mist that is gentle, warm, and full of unconditional love just for you.

6. Imagine yourself smiling inwardly as you breathe this golden mist of unconditional love up into your cranium, and say thank you to your brain for all its work.

7. Breathe in and smile more energy down into your cheeks and jaw, and feel your muscles relax. As the gentle

energy spreads, you may feel a warm glow or tingling, or simply a subtle but satisfying feeling internally as you follow the energy movement. Imagine using your eyes internally to look at your body parts and organs. You may want to consult the diagram at the end of this chapter for the location of your various organs. When I first started this meditation, I had no idea where some of my organs were located.

8. Continue breathing in and smile down into your neck and shoulders, allowing them to relax and giving thanks as the golden energy moves down.

9. Breathe deeply into your lungs and give thanks to your lungs for converting air into body energy.

10. Breathe and smile into your heart, and thank it for pumping your blood; allow a feeling of love and compassion to expand in your heart.

11. Smile down to all the other organs, including your liver on the right side under the rib cage, your spleen on the left side, stomach, large intestine, small intestine, and sexual organs. Take your time and relax. Smile into your thighs, all the way down to your toes. Give thanks

slowly and individually to each part of your body for its work. Keep smiling down and allow a feeling of unconditional love to spread all the way down to your feet. This practice will bring you to a centered place.

12. Then, most importantly, when the smile down is complete, take a relaxed breath and let your mind become quiet. This may be easier said then done. Many times, particularly in the beginning, you will feel fidgety or thoughts will keep coming into your mind. I lasted barely a minute the first time. When this occurs, acknowledge the thoughts and return, with a relaxed breath, to a quiet place after thanking your mind for sharing. When you feel complete, say thank you internally for the experience, get up, and go about your day or evening.

As you continue to do the practice, assuming you allow yourself the time and do not make it a pressured, must-do part of your day, you will find yourself learning to relax more easily and stay with the quiet time. When random thoughts intrude, acknowledge them and let them go on by. Do not get nervous about their appearance.

Their arrival is quite natural. Eventually you will find a deeper quiet. From this quiet internal space you may develop a great inner awareness, and now what appears as a thought will present itself as a new business idea or solution, or a revelation for a creative project. Furthermore, the smile down practice acts as an introduction to other practices. At times you may feel heat develop in your body, particularly your hands. This is quite normal and just indicates energy movement.

Once you are familiar with the smile down, you will find that you can reconnect to that centered space in a matter of seconds in the midst of a hectic day. Find a place where you won't be disturbed, close your eyes, and in five seconds you can be in touch with that quiet, centered space with a heightened awareness. The key here is to allow yourself the time to deepen your connection to yourself and the time to develop the feeling of love through your entire physical body. Literally smile down to each body part and thank it for its function, for each is a part of you—down to the warts.

When we have an ailment or hurt in our body, we

tend to disassociate ourselves from or feel anger toward those parts that are ill or ugly. When a child is sick, what do we do? We hug the child, kiss the part that hurts, whether it is a scrape on the knee or a case of the flu. Whatever it is, we give love to the child, which helps him heal. Give yourself the same thing. Embrace internally and give love to the physical or emotional part that hurts; it is part of you. Love it and encourage it to heal. Literally smile down unconditional love to each molecule. This practice, once you've done it a couple of times, will feel quite natural. You may wish to keep it short or allow yourself more time for greater depth, depending on your schedule. Sitting with a quiet mind at the completion is crucial. This is when deep revelations can well up. I will expand on this in later chapters, which will then enhance the practice. The key at the beginning is to gain greater awareness and centeredness while achieving a relaxed stance.

Achieving that stage of relaxed, heightened awareness in business action can be compared to a simple situation that we have all witnessed. A cat stalks and prepares to pounce on a piece of string. The cat will keep adjusting its body with increasingly heightened awareness. When it is in the final stages, that cat's awareness is fully focused, with its body centered and relaxed. It is only at the moment of decision and action that the cat fully tenses and releases with a full intent or commitment of energy to conclude the situation. I find that this metaphor relates to business decisions as well. With heightened awareness, I become centered yet relaxed while allowing parameters to shift until I am ready for decision and action. The meditations I describe here are designed to heighten your awareness and allow you to remain centered and relaxed.

As you heighten your awareness and get to know your physical body, its parts and rhythms, you will discover that your body communicates to you through gut reactions or other physical senses. The more in touch you are with yourself, the more you will notice how your body reacts to certain situations or people. Your body communicates with you all the time. Be aware of it and you will notice how it can help you make decisions and take action, or avoid inappropriate action in a business situation or in interpersonal communications.

In Summary

1. We start to heighten awareness through a breathing exercise.

2. The smile down meditation deepens the awareness by connecting to the physical body. Energy and feelings travel through the various parts of the body. Relaxation is important, also.

3. A quieted state provides the atmosphere for clarity of decision and significant revelations.

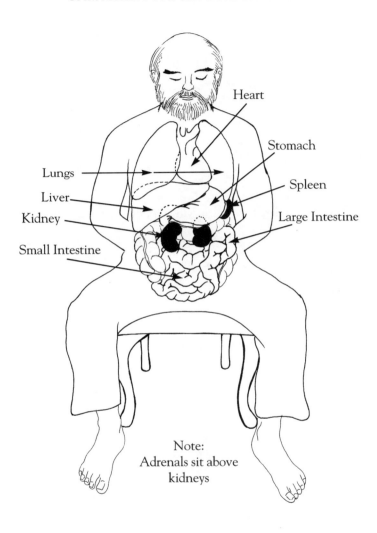

CHAPTER 2

BECOMING FULLY ENGAGED

Acting on a decision with full intent…

Have you ever had the experience of walking into a conference room with several people present and before you shake hands or say hello you get a clear sense that it will be either a difficult or an easy negotiation or meeting? How do you sense this information in your gut and then know it mentally and emotionally before anything transpires?

Let's explore this further. When you say, "I am Mary" or "John," who is speaking or what are you referring to? Is the "I" your body or your mind, or your body *and* your mind, or something altogether different? When you die and your body is laid out, is that physical mass really you? Is your personality present? Can you speak and laugh? No! So let me suggest that you are more than your physical form. Our bodies are the densest part of who we are, the slowest-vibrating aspect of our total being. Our bodies are the dense reflections of our subtler selves. Our subtler selves are the pieces of our being that resonate or vibrate at a higher frequency than our bodies. These vibrations are the connection between our physical manifestation and Universal Knowledge. If you pay close attention to the first instance of your waking process from dream time, you may notice that your body seems to have a higher vibratory rate. This vibration is our connection to Universal Knowledge, which is more easily perceived during our transition from sleep to full waking. Let us return to that meeting in the conference room. Your subtle energies, or the subtle vibratory part of you, have picked up the energies, or vibrations, of the other people present. Your extended antenna, or the subtle consciousness within you, has received an implied message. Your physical body interprets and reacts to it, and you act accordingly.

When we practice the smile down (chapter 1), we

experience how our bodies feel and react when we use subtle energies in meditation. It appears that as we become more in tune with our bodies we will also become more connected to Universal Knowledge and the energies and emotions affecting us and, in turn, we will learn to be clearer, more in tune, with actions or decisions we implement. The more aware and consciously connected we are to ourselves, and thereby to Universal Knowledge, the more easily we can come to clear decisions and actions (i.e., the message in the conference room). We can easily and graciously make the right decisions and take the right actions in business. We should be aware, however, that right decisions and right action do not necessarily guarantee the outcome our mind has preconceived. The key is to be clear about the direction we want to take, without holding on to regrets or looking back, and to allow the outcome to manifest.

Buddhists have written volumes about "right action," yet nowhere is it really described. In teaching spiritual practices, I like to use the example of certain Zen Buddhist Roshis (a Roshi is a master, or spiritual teacher). In

Zen practice, much time is spent in sitting meditation to deepen one's awareness and hopefully reach higher states of consciousness. Many times, a Roshi will give the student a riddle or mental puzzle (called a *koan*) that has no apparent answer or solution. The student will work on this riddle in meditation and then from time to time meet with the Roshi, who examines his student's progress. The Roshi may, if deeming the moment right, slap the student across the face to assist his awakening. The student may experience a sudden surge of energy and awaken to a deep part of self to gain insight into true being. The student's consciousness will have been greatly expanded. I tell my class that if I went around to each one and slapped them in the face, I probably would end up with a lot of lawsuits. So what makes the Roshi's slap a "right action" and my hypothetical act a potential lawsuit? Right action comes out of a heightened awareness of the particular situation and a higher consciousness of all the parameters—people, money, time, ethics—involved in a decision-making process. Therefore, right action cannot be standardized into a code of behavior that is applied indiscriminately.

Without clarity in our decision-making, we cannot expect to have right action and be successful in business. I believe that if enough facts are available to us, the decision is usually made for us. However, most of our major decisions are made without enough facts. So what prompts us to take one direction or another? Is it intuition, vibes, gut reaction, self-doubt—either induced by others or by oneself? Apparently these doubts reflect a split in our being, one part of our mind arguing against a desire of another part of ourselves. How do we achieve total clarity, a full intent on our part to move in a particular direction? Full intent is a way to describe our urge or passion, our full will, to make a decision and then act on it. Full will involves all that we are—physical, mental, emotional, our consciousness. Without that full commitment, full will, chances are good you will fall flat on your face (not that there is anything wrong with this, for failure is a great teacher). Let us now explore how to completely engage so we can have clarity in our decisions and actions.

By starting at the beginning, we can attempt to understand the split within: that of the self and doubt. Right from birth we have an ego. The minute we come out of the birth canal we are in shock, not just physically from the bright lights and cold, but spiritually. We are pure soul or spirit that has manifested physically and we carry with us knowledge from more subtle realms. We are shocked because what we find when we see our parents and other beings is quite different from our knowledge. In that single second our ego is split. We create a false self, or false ego, to protect the true self or true ego. I sometimes refer to this false ego as the babysitter, for it has only one purpose and that is to protect your deepest core, your true self.

Contrary to many stereotypical new-age thinkers, I do not agree that you have to give up your ego to expand your consciousness and refine your vibrations, your intuition, your knowing. Indeed, we need our egos to operate on the earth plane. The question we need to address is that of the relationship of the true ego to the false ego and how to get them to work in concert, for surely you cannot give one up in favor of the other; they are both a part of you.

Our true self is that part of us that, on a spiritual level, is still connected to Universal Knowledge and wants to act spontaneously, with no hidden agendas. Our true self wants to be open and honest and to experience all the energies that manifest in our physical experience. The false self, or babysitter, believes that openness of the true self or ego can lead to pain on a physical, mental, or emotional level, and therefore the false ego strives to protect the true ego from that pain—not understanding or accepting the fact that many times it is through our vulnerabilities, our hurts, that we gain knowledge and develop our consciousness and wisdom. Unfortunately, over time the false ego gains greater importance and thinks it is in charge. To adapt to the outside world, the false ego creates masks to handle situations, protecting the true ego but hiding who we really are. We talk and present ourselves one way to our boss, another way to our children, and still another way at cocktail parties.

A few years ago I got a call from a dear friend, Alan, who was lamenting his job loss. I was visiting the seashore of Long Island and invited him to take a long walk with me on the beach. As we walked and talked I told Alan that what I perceived from the conversation seemed to be a case of misrepresentation—the false ego or false self taking over from the true self. I reflected to Alan that when he went for a job interview his false ego presented a man who was very agreeable, a yes-man who did not question or contradict any company policy. Yet once in a position, his intelligence and decisiveness brought innovation and growth to any job and also threatened those around him. Soon his superiors would either fire him or make work unbearable so he would quit. I suggested that had his fear of rejection not gotten in the way of presenting his true self at the beginning, he might have aligned his talents and abilities with a boss and company that appreciated his potential. I encouraged Alan to be in touch and express his true self fully at all times in any business relationship. Alan eventually came to the conclusion that his true self could flourish only in his own business. Four years later his business is thriving and he is enjoying life on all levels.

We are so used to presenting our false self, or false ego, to please others, obtain their approval, and make them like us, that we often find it difficult to develop a clear, full intent for our decisions and actions. To be effective in our business life we need full intent, the cooperation of false and true ego. The false ego, or as the Zen Buddhists call it, the monkey mind, is always chattering and questioning our motives and intent. How do we distinguish this chatter and questioning of false ego from our true ego and intent? This is a difficult question because some hesitation or questioning is valid and comes from our true self evaluating a situation. The true self is connected to Universal Knowledge and is trying to communicate, usually through our body, our belly brain, that it is perceiving a situation that is different from what the false ego is reacting to in the outer world. In Western society we have been brought up to believe that the mind is everything, and we have, for the most part, lost our trust in our inner core, our true self, which manifests subtly in our bodies. Practices such as the smile down and other meditations are a means of restoring both the trust and our intrinsic connection to the true self. They also increase our awareness so that we can distinguish our true self more clearly and act according to its wishes.

Merging the true and false egos can be challenging. Once, when I was an assistant project manager in a design and construction firm doing paper mill and steel mill projects, I began working late hours to both learn new concepts and realize completion of projects since the company, with an unexpected excess of contracts, had overloaded our team. In the midst of this hectic schedule my true ego decided that I wished to pursue a master's degree in business administration. This was before any spiritual work, but in retrospect I now understand the dynamics involved.

Deep within, at a gut level, I wanted to get an MBA to further myself and reach top levels of management. As soon as I contemplated this decision my false ego, or monkey mind, came in to raise doubts to protect my true self. "You are already working late hours and will be exhausted! You have a family with two young sons who need you! You will be taking away creative working time from your job and might not advance as fast." And so forth.... An internal conflict or split developed between the true and false egos. While the false ego tried to protect the true self, in actuality it created self-doubt and was undermining. I forced a decision on my false ego to go ahead with the educational plans, creating internal tension that manifested in external conflict with my family and at work. Now, understanding the process, I might invite the false ego through meditation to the decision-making. This would involve having an internal conversation with my false ego and exploring the point of contention. Further reasoning with the false self would include how I might cut back my hours at work and justify to the boss that the new knowledge and expertise would in the long run be of greater benefit to the company. In order to reduce tension in my family I might extend the MBA schooling from three to four years. By going over each point with the false ego, I would be able to unify the split and then move forward with full intent and a passion to pursue the MBA.

If you are not fully together—have your full intent invested in a decision—the outcome will not be successful. So how do we engage our full intent in a business action, or in any context? We cannot suppress or disown our false ego, as I did originally, any more than we can suppress or disown our heart or lungs. The consequences of suppression produce increasing tension, which often leads to disaster, in my case a heart attack. All the pieces make up our whole. So how do we deal with pieces of ourselves that we have difficulty with? We need to *allow* our false ego and then *invite* it to be fully part of ourselves. Bring the false ego to consciousness. Have an internal conversation with it. I do not suggest that you mumble to yourself, moving your lips as some street people do, as this might not go over too well in the corporate world. But I do advise a point-by-point, internal conversation with your false ego. Since the false ego can be quite clever and logical, ask it to be involved in the decision. The false ego frequently has valid points, which is why you need to invite it to the decision and ask it to help you resolve the objections. You might even give it a name so it feels like a familiar old friend. Once your false ego has begun to see the advantages of the course of action, you can ask it to trust your consciousness and deep self in that this will be beneficial, and then go ahead and invite all of you— including your false ego—to the party, to the fun, to the passion of decision and action. When you have answered the chatter of monkey mind or false ego, then you are all together; the physical and emotional will feel complete and you will be making a decision with full intent. As we develop further meditation practices and you work with them, you will come to feel and recognize that clarity of action emanates from the belly brain, or gut, and you will become much more attuned to the communications that are coming into you for processing and evaluation.

An important aspect of the dynamic between true and false self is the response to fear. Fear in its initial stage at the body level is a communication from true self, a message from Universal Knowledge. At a more esoteric level, fear is a manifestation of our separation from Universal Knowledge and our inability to trust the unseen connection. Fear is a clear communication from the true self that indicates a hesitation or lack of clarity. There is no understanding of a solution or direction to be taken. In my MBA experience I heard only the chatter of monkey mind or the false self. The feeling of fear or the true self sending up a red flag was not evident. The vibration of fear in our body concerning a business decision is an important emotion; it usually alerts us to something that is amiss. Most often, fear's communication gets distorted by our monkey mind. The initial alert by true self gets lost in the "what ifs" of the false ego. As one of my spiritual teachers would say, "Bite off the head of fear and make it your partner, for it has great energy." By using the energy of fear we approach the union of our selves, true and false egos, and the reconnection to Universal Knowledge. This reconnection can then help us come to full intent and into action. This concept was brought home to me when I was hanging on a ledge at seventeen thousand feet in Tibet, on one of my spiritual quests. I could fall and become paralyzed or engage my fear—the construct of monkey mind—and move forward to survive and complete my journey (the chosen path).

Let us look at fear through a personal business experience. In the last years before I sold my coffee company, we were offered and subsequently accepted large amounts of coffee coming from an unusual source. At the time, we checked all the documentation and information we could because of the size of the deal and the promise of an unusually large profit. This appeared to be a case where all the facts were present and a decision was a foregone conclusion. Yet my gut was sending out signals of fear. All the traders met on the issue and everyone wanted to go ahead with the deal. Internally, I overruled the unmistakable fear emanating from true self. This proved to be a mistake. When the coffee arrived in the United States our shipments, along with those of several competitors, were detained by the United States customs on the grounds that the origins of the coffee did not agree with the labeling on the bags, a false representation. My company and I experienced much aggravation and financial loss when I denied my fear (the true self). As a result, substantial expenses were incurred in order to reach a settlement with customs, shippers, and the re-exportation of the coffee. The important lesson was that I always listen to my belly brain. During this time of extreme stress and tension, the spiritual practices kept me centered and relaxed enough to develop full intent in coming to a solution with all concerned.

In Summary

1. We continually receive communication from Universal Knowledge.

2. We need to heighten our awareness in our whole being to receive and be clear about communication from Universal Knowledge.

3. True ego represents our true self, our intended desires and needs, while false ego manifests as the protector to avoid pain to the true ego.

4. Fear serves as a communication and a warning that something needs careful observation. The energy of fear can offer union of true and false self and connection to Universal Knowledge.

4. Full intent for decisions and actions can be developed by having the true ego and false ego in agreement after

communication from Universal Knowledge.

A verse from the Upanishad, translated by Deepak Chopra, expresses this dynamic succinctly:

You are what your deep, driving desire is.
As your desire is, so is your will.
As your will is, so is your deed.
As your deed is, so is your destiny.

—Brihadaranyaka Upanishad IV. 4.5

CHAPTER 3

UNDERSTANDING RESISTANCE: THE LAW OF OCTAVES

. . . the hero's first threshold guardian

I enjoy racing sailboats. When a sailboat is in the groove, moving at full speed in the desired direction, the feeling is exhilarating and the movement effective and efficient. When a puff of wind comes along that is greater than the base breeze, the hull develops resistance through the water. You could call this the first threshold of resistance, when the crew must quickly adjust the sails and helm to bring the boat into effective and efficient movement. You can feel a new surge, particularly in the helm. You might say the boat has shifted to a higher gear or vibration.

Sometimes, particularly in smaller boats, the vessel can be overpowered as the wind continues to build. The sailboat will keep coming up on its side, at an extreme angle of heel, to the point where it will go over. In the instant before capsizing, there is a lull when everything seems to stand still; that indicates a gap or resistance beyond the crew's control. During the moment of lull, if the crew lets go of the sails and trusts the outcome, usually the boat will start righting itself. The crew then needs to readjust the sail and helm to move forward once again in a groove corrected for speed. There is a definite feeling at the moment just before the potential capsize of depowering the boat and truly surrendering the sails. The sensation is a combination of anguish, hope for a good outcome, and a feeling of surrender, knowing that the outcome is beyond one's control.

So what does this have to do with business? I use this example because it is clear that in the physical world of sailboat racing, the boat and crew go through changes of tempo, some resistances, and an adjustment of gears. The same thing happens in any business. In more esoteric terms, the resistance and changes might be said to reflect what is known as the Law of Octaves, which operates throughout the universe. Let us use a simple point of reference that most of us are familiar with, the musical scale. I will try to illustrate this in the broadest, most familiar concept, the musical scale *do-re-mi-fa-so-la-ti,* and then the next octave higher starting again with *do.* If you listen to a scale you may perceive a slight shift following *do-re-mi*—a change between *mi* and the next note, *fa.* The notes *do-re-mi* represent full steps, with a sharp or black key between *do* and *re,* then *re* and *mi.* But no sharp exists between *mi* and *fa,* resulting in a half step or compression between the two. This change exemplifies the first threshold of resistance within an octave. Once the threshold has been surmounted, the scale continues, *fa-so-la-ti;* then a second and much more significant resistance, or in this case a gap, is encountered and must be breached before the next higher octave—starting with *do*—can be reached. Again, we experience a half step or absent black key, but we also move up to another octave, in theory, on and on indefinitely.

If we pay close attention to the everyday happenings in business, as in the sailing metaphor, we will note that much activity seems to follow the same pattern as the musical scale. We all come up with new ideas, solutions, or projects within our business environment, or with ideas for an altogether new business. We move forward with these new concepts, the *do-re-mi* of the scale, and then suddenly we hit resistance. This is the first threshold before the *fa*. At this point, if we do not input energy and hold a full intent to move forward our project will fail. If you look around you, you will often see people getting enthusiastic about new projects and moving full steam ahead only to quit or back away at that first threshold of resistance. This pattern has been observed throughout human history and prehistory.

Joseph Campbell refers to that first resistance in *The Power of Myth* as the hero's first "threshold guardian" on his journey. Some people are never able to get through the first resistance and therefore repeat *do-re-mi* without ever reaching the *fa*. For example, a person continually starts new business projects but is never able to follow through to completion. It is important to note here that we should not always assume we need to break through the resistance. Sometimes our true self is signaling the body with a feeling of tension or apprehension, the sense that something is not right. Then developing our full intent means to stop short and back away from our project. The monkey mind may have constructed some fantastic scheme of great success and vast riches. The true self knows this is pie in the sky. The belly brain is communicating difficulty, although at that moment the body can give no justification to the mind. Very likely you have had this experience at some time and gone ahead with a business project that totally failed or backfired later. When the failure happened and you looked back and understood why the project failed, you probably kicked yourself for not having followed your intuition.

You need full intent to move forward through or to back away from the first resistance. I emphasize that at this threshold you need to be decisive, because otherwise you will never develop clarity and know when to commit or stop. Listen to your belly, heighten your awareness of the subtle communications you receive from Universal Knowledge, and develop full intent to move forward or back away. In keeping with the circular scheme of these practices, it is important to remember that heightened awareness and full intent through meditation fine-tune the decision-making process.

Let us assume that you have developed full intent, bridged the first resistance, and are successfully moving ahead in your project through the rest of the octave, *fa-so-la-ti*, much like the sailboat adjusting for the higher puffs of wind. You now have experience and know how to line up true and false ego and develop full intent. You pour your energy into the project to bridge the gap from *ti* to *do* in the next octave, but nothing happens. You call in experts, sink in more money, do computer analysis, yet nothing comes to fruition. Why? This next gap is not within your sphere of control. This octave threshold is the place of surrender to a higher consciousness, to Universal Knowledge. This is the place where the boat is near capsize and you need to depower. It would appear that business as well as all creation moves in patterns similar to the Law of Octaves. That pattern is in harmonic relation to the energy emanating from Universal Knowledge. At this point, only trust and a deep, inner knowing will guide you to the best outcome. I will describe several examples of this process.

A pivotal illustration of the Law of Octaves occurred in my own business life in 1975, before I was on a spiritual path. I believe my intuition was somewhat developed since my success in the commodity world was well on its way, but I had no understanding of the consciousness and energy of octaves. I was not consciously in touch with the Universal Knowledge being communicated through my belly brain and, as in this instance, did not always listen or trust that feeling.

In Kinshasa, Zaire, now called Democratic Republic of Congo, the government coffee director, a good friend of mine from whom I bought a lot of coffee, was politically removed in 1975 after two years in this position, a typical turn of events in African affairs. He was replaced by a man named Ndaka, one of then-President Mobutu's protègès, who had been head of the secret police. I tried to make an appointment with Ndaka by phone and telex from New York, to no avail. Unbeknownst to me, I was finding the first resistance in the octave. I wanted a large coffee contract, and with a sense of determination or full intent, I immediately flew to Kinshasa. I still could not get an appointment and was told to negotiate with Ndaka's assistant, bridging the first resistance. The assistant director was charming, everything went smoothly, and he agreed to sell me a large amount of coffee subject to Ndaka's review; the *fa-so-la-ti* portion of the octave. Several days went by and I was unable to meet with Ndaka or get a confirmation on my contract. I had completed *fa-so-la-ti* and had reached the threshold or gap of the next octave. This is where I should have let go and surrendered to the higher forces of the universe. I did not understand the feeling of anguish and emptiness, and the need to surrender. I flew out of Zaire to Europe for some meetings, and during that time Brazil had the worst coffee frost in its history. The loss of the Brazilian crop guaranteed major price increases and high coffee demand from roasters. I had to get the Zairian coffee. I could not accept failure, and believed I could overcome any difficulty, even though I experienced anguish and fear from my belly brain. I flew back to Zaire to find that the United States ambassador had been asked to leave and all American multiple-entry visas had been canceled. This meant I could not legally enter the country after landing. Again, I could not embrace lack of success; I did not understand I was at the end of the octave resistance threshold, so I continued to fight instead of waiting for an outcome. I persisted by bribing an official to get into the country. I definitely was not in tune with the belly brain and pattern of Universal Knowledge. Now I was in serious trouble. I was in Zaire illegally at a time when Americans were not welcome. The American Embassy could not help. Ndaka, after finally meeting with me, told me he would let me know about the contract before leaving the country the next day. After pulling all the strings I could, I was able to straighten out my passport and get out of Zaire. After two months I received a small contract that was never fulfilled by Zaire. If I had understood my body's messages, and been aware of Universal Knowledge and the Law of Octaves, I would have saved myself much aggravation and money.

As the years passed and I worked on developing my consciousness, I came to understand and act on these important spiritual principles. In November of 1996, my second book, *Strong Brew*, had just been published. A friend of mine introduced me to a woman named Pamela who was a staff reporter for the *Los Angeles Times*. My friend had explained to Pamela what my book was about, and she had shown interest in considering it for a story. The *do-re-mi* of this octave had gone well. Now I hit the first resistance in the octave: I was unable to connect with her by phone. I flew to Los Angeles for some radio shows I had been booked on and was still unable to reach her. I knew I was in the threshold guardian of the octave and therefore invested my full intent and renewed my efforts to reach Pamela. Finally, after playing phone tag, we connected and she explained that her daughter had just broken her arm and she had been too preoccupied to return my calls. She suggested having lunch the next day. The threshold had been breached. We had a delightful lunch, during which she interviewed me and made copious notes. The *fa-so-la-ti* of the octave was proceeding well. As we were finishing lunch, Pamela informed me she liked my story but could not guarantee an article, as she was not one of the book reviewers and would have to get her editor's approval for a story. At this juncture, I realized I had reached the final resistance point of the octave. I felt the anguish of wanting my story in the *Los Angeles Times* and also an emptiness in my gut. I knew this is where I had to surrender to the higher forces of the universe to bring forth whatever was in my best interest. I could have gone and done handstands in front of the *Times* building to get my story in print, but this would have been to no avail. I surrendered to spirit and waited to see whether the gap would be bridged to the higher octave and my article would be printed, or another outcome would be presented. Two weeks later, my book and I were mentioned on the front page of the "Living" section of the *Los Angeles Times*.

Commodity trading charts all have the same patterns, whether the chart covers one minute, one day, one month, or one year. The same is true about octaves; they apply whether the task is a small one or a large multi-year project. In other words, the patterns are repetitive no matter their magnitude. You need to decide which to focus on, similar to a short- or long-term trader. As you become conscious of octaves and where you are in their unfolding, you will develop a sense of how, when, and where to use your energy to achieve the best results in a business environment.

In Summary

1. We have emphasized the importance of heightening your awareness, your belly brain communication of Universal Knowledge.

2. We have become acquainted with the Law of Octaves, the pattern of the energy emanating from Universal Knowledge.

3. We have examined resistance and how this operates in the patterned scheme called octaves:

a. As you become aware of where you are with the movement of the energy as it relates to the octave, be conscious of your behavior patterns. If challenged at the first threshold, develop full intent either to break through or to back away, depending on the communication from belly brain.

b. If you determine you are at the second gap where the octave ends, trust and surrender to Universal Knowledge that it will present the best outcome.

CHAPTER 4

USING THE LIFE FORCE

. . .your desire must be realistic in terms of your belief system

From studying with various spiritual teachers, I have come to understand that the life force is the conscious energy of Universal Knowledge or, in Western terms, it is God's love that is everywhere and permeates everything. Seemingly, the life force is a triune dynamic force that will support and guide us through our life if we are prepared to allow ourselves the connection and then adjust to it. As the designation implies, triune refers to three aspects: the feminine attributes, the masculine attributes, and the dynamic balance of the two working together. In order to understand these three forces, I will again use my favorite sport, sailing, as a metaphor.

Picture a large sailboat racing out to sea. What are the dynamics of the life force? The wind is pushing hard against the sails, trying to tilt the boat over. This represents the masculine side of the life force. The water is resisting the push against the keel and the hull of the boat. This represents the female side of the life force. If the crew on board did nothing after setting the original course, the boat would lose its balance and either go in circles, tip over, or crash ashore. The key is that the crew adjusts the sails and helm of the boat to keep it on course at the most effective speed through the water. I say "effective" because many conditions can arise, from calm wind and waters which would call for much sail, to heavy wind and rough seas which would demand shortened sail and adjusted helm. When the boat is in balance it will effectively drive forward at full speed to its destination. That balance, which is not static but very vibrant, is the result of the masculine and feminine forces working together to move the boat forward. This will be referred to as the dynamic balance, or neutral force.

This same concept applies to our everyday business activities and to our everyday life. We are continually buffeted by the winds and waves of business vagaries, and it is our job either as a crew member or helmsman of the business to adjust operations, decisions, and directions so we can most effectively navigate the wind and waters of commerce. When some situation in the business environment is out of balance, such as the invention by a competitor of a better widget than ours, or when we cannot determine the balance, for example, when cost overruns erode profits, then the business or the individual will be thrown off-kilter until that neutral point is found. Sometimes this imbalance can be most unpleasant. The boat might capsize because the crew has not adjusted to the dynamic forces. Similarly, the company may go bankrupt as those responsible are unable to perceive the corresponding dynamic forces.

Let us look at this in a simple way. Imagine Universal Knowledge as a huge battery with one terminal positive, or male, and the other terminal negative, or female. When the two terminals are connected, electrical current flows, representing the dynamic force of the battery, or the resulting link of the male and female poles. This is the dynamic balance or neutral force that always seeks to close the connection between the female and male energies. In Taoist terms, this dynamic is represented by the yin/yang symbol, the dark and the light intertwined in a circle symbolizing the balance or neutral force. Within the symbol is a dot of white positioned in the black and a dot of black within the white, indicating that each contains something of the other. The same is true of ourselves—male nature within woman and female nature within man; we are never purely one kind of energy. So we seek in our partners, consciously or subconsciously, the balance to the various poles of energy within us to try and reach the neutral balance to close the connection. Similarly, in business the energy always seeks closure, the attainment of dynamic balance or the neutral force. When I speak of the life force, I mean all three components.

The male side of the life force can be described as expansive, pushing, warm, or even hot; white or light in color; associated with daytime and rising. It is best summarized as the positive propulsive. The female side of the life force is contracting, pulling, cool, or even cold; dark or black in color; associated with nighttime and descending. It is best summarized as the negative attractive. This is why, in general, we are best suited for activity during the positive propulsive daytime part of the twenty-four-hour cycle, and the negative attractive nighttime is best suited for rest, receiving, dream time, and the repair of our mental, physical, and emotional selves.

As I have said, the life force will always—repeat *always*—seek that neutral point, which is the place where all three forces are in balance. When I refer to the neutral *force* I mean the resultant dynamic balance of the positive propulsive and negative attractive. This can mean balanced movement or total stillness. The neutral *point* is achieved when you know everything is working satisfactorily in your business activities. You have reached balance either in movement or stasis. Depending on conditions, there are many potential neutral points for the decisions we make. Every business decision we conceive or action we take has an infinite number of potential outcomes depending on the various outside forces affecting the situation. The life force will take in all the opposing energies to bring the outcome to a dynamic balance and neutral point, whether or not we desire it or think it is fair.

Let us explore how we might use, or rather ask for help from, the life force in a business decision by splitting the life force into its separate components. The intentional conjuring of the life force in this manner is called a conflictive meditation. These individual components can be identified as positive propulsive and negative attractive. This splitting action will cause the opposite poles of the life force to want to rush together, seeking closure in order to create the neutral force. To explain this fully, I will give a hypothetical example and then actual illustrations from my business experiences. Let us assume that you have reached the age of retirement and want to sell your business. After you have taken appropriate action to create the result you want, such as listing the business with brokers or in the paper, sit down in a meditation posture as outlined in the smile down (chapter 1). Place both feet on the ground, straighten your back, put your tongue against the roof of your mouth, relax your shoulders, and tuck your chin slightly in so your head is straight and lined up with your spine. Then put your left hand in your lap, palm up, right hand clasped over left, palm down, and close your eyes with a smile in them. Relax.

To be successful in this meditation, when you are asking the life force for something, you must connect fully to each aspect of the life force. You may start with either the negative or positive aspects. In our example we will start with the feminine, or negative attractive, and in meditation assume these feminine qualities of attraction or what the needs are, concentrating on the emotional aspect. In order to transmit a message to the life force, you must invest yourself fully in this core desire or need that you have for your business. Experience the feeling at its innermost depth, not just as a mental exercise. Be as specific as possible. This might reflect the dollar amount you feel the business is worth and the time frame for its sale. Let us assume you would like a million dollars for your business and you would like to sell it within the next nine months. You need to visualize in detail the various components of your business that you are selling—machines, buildings, capital, and people, all that would stay with the operation. I must emphasize that you have to be fully vested in the desired sale and really *feel* your requirement for the money, really develop that feminine quality of attraction and connect with it. While you sit in your meditative posture, picture your needs in detail and with emotion, and hold that picture on one side of your body or mind.

Once you feel that you have stabilized the negative attractive in its visualized and emotional state, move your attention to the other side of your body or mind and create the positive propulsive image through the masculine side, or yang aspect. That is, activate the complementary energies in the world that are needed to make the sale happen. The positive propulsive might consist of picturing many people looking in papers and calling brokers, actively trying to find a business just like yours. You can picture these people with checkbooks in hand really wanting to buy. Again, you must invest yourself fully in this male energy of pushing, aggressively searching for a business like yours. You need to develop this picture of the positive propulsive totally and separately from the negative attractive picture.

The key to the meditation is to bring both potentials, the positive propulsive and the negative attractive, to a dual climax *without ever connecting the two*. It is necessary to become each aspect of the situation separately. That is, you must *not* picture actually selling your business, the actual consummation of the sale, because to do so would short-circuit the life force that is seeking the dynamic balance or neutral force. Remember that the life force is always seeking a dynamic balance at any level, so if you *yourself* provide the energy of closure for the sale, the dynamic balance will have already been achieved and the life force will not act on your request. In Judeo-Christian terms, God will not answer your prayers. For this meditation to work as a request, it is essential to fully embrace both components of the life force without connecting the two opposites to create the third, the neutral force.

Since you will be unable to engage the opposite sides of the life force at the same time, you need to learn to switch rapidly between the two poles. First develop either the negative attractive or the positive propulsive on one side, then quickly go to the other side and develop the opposite. As you strongly create each situation and then continually flip back and forth between the two poles, you will find that a vibration develops between them. Your body will generate a feeling of excitement and internal energy. The more you can connect to the picture and the emotions of each side and rapidly switch from one to the other, the greater the vibrations and the faster they will develop. Eventually the vibrations will develop such a fast and intense rhythm that you will not be able to hold them. With a grand surge the two will collapse together. This experience might be compared to an orgasm as the apex is reached and then the energy falls to a quiet state. At this point you will know that the communication has been transmitted to the life force. When you become familiar with the practice you will find the vibration quite high and you may experience a sense of sexual arousal. This is quite normal as you near the collapsing of the opposite poles of the life force into the neutral force for its completion.

A few words follow about the necessary conditions for doing a conflictive meditation. First of all, this practice will not work unless your goal is consistent with your belief system. If you believe your business is only worth half a million, the life force will not respond if you ask to receive a million for it. Similarly, your time frame and your desire must be realistic in terms of your belief system. If half of you is nostalgic about your wonderful business and not prepared to let go and move forward with a sale, the life force will sense your lack of energy or commitment, and nothing will happen. An important caution concerning this practice: it must never be used to affect someone else's free will. As we deepen our knowledge, heighten our awareness, develop our consciousness, and learn how to recognize and affect outcomes using certain spiritual practices, we must also take full responsibility for ourselves and our actions. Not only does manipulating someone else's free will have potentially serious ethical implications on this earth plane, but for those who believe our souls are immortal, it will have serious karmic implications. The development of the power of our consciousness, whether used in conflictive meditation or other spiritual practices, must entail responsibility to ourselves and to all that is part of our planet. The greater our consciousness, knowledge, and wisdom, the greater our responsibility.

I can illustrate this point more clearly with the story of a friend who had full intent, but with reservations in his belief system. As a consulting electrical engineer, he was having a difficult time making ends meet. He did a conflictive meditation to win the New Jersey Lottery, a positive propulsive act, in order to solve his financial needs, the negative attractive aspect. Winning the lottery was not consistent with his belief system as a means of earning a living, so this did not come to pass. However, his full intent and his need for money, the negative attractive, were so great that the life force substituted a positive propulsive that was consistent with his belief system: it provided him with six calls the next day for lucrative consulting jobs that alleviated his financial problems.

Two years ago I was teaching conflictive meditation in Santa Fe, New Mexico. We had been experiencing an extremely dry spell, which resulted in many forest fires. We decided as a group to do a conflictive meditation for rain. We established a time frame for occurrence within the next three weeks, which everyone could accept. We pictured vividly the parched earth desiring rain, the neg-ative attractive. Unfortunately, we were not specific enough about the amount, and did not picture the details of a great storm but only heavy clouds with moisture, the positive propulsive. We had not put enough energy into the male side, a big storm. However, we did get several hours of rain three days later, which helped to lessen the arid conditions.

On a more personal level, I was anxious to sell a vaca-tion home in New York State that I no longer could visit often since I had moved to the Southwest. I did a con-flictive meditation, setting a time frame of one year. I knew that I had deep attachments to the house because of many fond memories involving vacations, family, friends, and wonderful, relaxed meditations. A month went by without any activity on the house. I realized I had to clear my belief system of my attachments before I could develop full intent and do a successful conflictive meditation. I went around to each room, corridor, and the grounds, stood for a moment picturing the memories and then claiming them as my own, realizing that the sale would only be of brick, mortar, and land. I committed my full intent in the manner I described in the example of selling a business. I sold the house two months later.

One last comment. When you use conflictive meditation you are asking or expressing a desire, much as in prayer, that the life force provide you with a closure. This desire must reflect all of you, your full commitment. It is never a demand or expectation, for this would not transmit the negative attractive, the *pulling* of what you desire toward you. You need to invest all of yourself, particularly the emotional aspect of your desire. Interestingly enough, over the years of practicing this meditation I have discovered that communication with the life force seems to be easier for me at sea level than at high altitudes. When I really want to work on a project, I find I can more easily conjure the life force at lower altitudes even when the issue or project is to be activated at higher altitudes.

A note of caution: If this tool is used for negative purposes it will either not produce results or it will unleash forces that you will regret having contacted. The conflictive meditation, through which you are asking the life force to help you with an outcome, is a powerful tool and must be used in full consciousness for the betterment of business, self, and planet.

In Summary

1. The life force, the current of Universal Knowledge, is a triune force made up of the feminine and masculine attributes as well as the neutral force.

2. The life force always seeks the neutral point represented by a dynamic balance.

3. In a conflictive meditation we split the life force into

its positive propulsive and negative attractive components to seek help in resolving a business situation.

4. Awareness of extraneous issues or conflicting emotions are essential to ensure success in the practice.

CHAPTER 5

GOING DEEPER

You are in charge and must decide your priorities

Thus far, we have developed a heightened awareness with an understanding of how to engage full intent for conflictive meditation in order to function more effectively in business. Our next and most important step is to plug ourselves directly into the life force through meditation. The key here is to use our *free will* to align ourselves with the flow of the life force and to thereby move in the most graceful way through life. In Western terms, "not my will but thy will" expresses not a subjugation to the Goddess/God but an allowance on our part to let Universal Knowledge manifest the best of who we are. For instance, picture yourself driving a car on a winding road. Now imagine Universal Knowledge designating this winding road as a personal life force path for your purpose on earth. Your free will determines how you handle the road. You could decide to be conservative and drive at fifteen miles an hour and, therefore, take a long time to reach your destination. Or you could drive at one hundred miles an hour and crash on a curve, missing your destination. As a third possibility, you might use your free will to determine how fast and with what control you negotiate the road, the path of the life force, guided by the road's condition and your abilities. Unfortunately, in the case of the life force path we do not always have big yellow signs suggesting the speed or foretelling the curves ahead. Once we can connect to the life force directly we will become a clearer conduit for Universal Knowledge and be more definitive in our business practices. This connection will impact many aspects of our lives. Likewise, tapping into Universal Knowledge will enhance the work we have already done in the previous chapters.

My first experience in connecting to the life force through meditation occurred in Chinatown, New York, while sitting with a Taoist master. Within a week of practicing every day I had a clear message from Universal

Knowledge. I needed to sell my importing business and move on to other ventures. At the time I supposed it might be a construct of my mind, but quickly the certainty of the situation could be felt quite clearly. I pressed forward with the concept. To my astonishment, my partner agreed to this action and within a year we had closed a deal for the business transfer.

At first, this meditation may seem quite complicated, but in actuality it is simple. The most difficult part of the meditation is memorizing the different components. Once memorized, the meditation elements can be realized quite easily. In Appendix A, I have provided a quick reference that you can use as a guide after reading through and understanding the meditation in its entirety. An analogy might be made to the programming of a computer where, once complete, the click of one icon unfolds a whole program. To accomplish a life force connection meditation we must first ask the monkey mind, or false ego, to help us direct the energy. That is, we must be ready to move wholly into this meditation. We need to immerse fully in the process.

There are three parts to this meditation. The first involves the positive propulsive flow, which starts at the navel with a *pushing* action and moves down the center line of the front of the torso to the bottom of the torso, continuing around and then up the spine in back, and over the head, reconnecting at the navel. The flow always starts and ends at the navel. The second part, the negative attractive, is a *pulling* action that moves in exactly the opposite direction, with the starting point again at the navel. Both aspects of the life force must be used equally to be in balance and to connect to the third part of the meditation, the neutral force. During the third part of the meditation, when we sit with quiet minds, the neutral force manifests. A drawing of the meditation posture with the energy points is located at the end of the chapter.

Since this meditation requires familiarity with the body's anatomy, I will describe each point referred to before guiding you through the process. The illustration at the end of this chapter shows you the locations. I am going to discuss in detail the characteristics of each center, since the main purpose is to open the points of energy or windows to different aspects of the life force in order to increase our connection to the life force and our consciousness. The more open we are to the flow of the life force, the clearer we will be in everything we do and the greater our consciousness and wisdom, for the life force has a consciousness beyond our greatest imaginings.

Point 1 - Navel:

The navel, the center or window of balance for all our energies. When this window is properly open and the energies are flowing easily, we will always feel in balance. When the navel window is not fully flowing, we will feel off balance or out of tune.

Point 2 - Sexual Center:

For *women:* If you place your hands in an open heart shape with the point of the thumbs together at the navel and index fingers touching, your pinkies should be over your ovaries. Your sexual center will be halfway between the two.

For *men:* The sexual center will be at the base of the penis. *Everyone:* This center, or window, is the center of creativity. After all, when two people come together and produce a child, what greater creativity exists! When the sexual window energies flow we can be at our most creative. Many times when someone has a creative thought they will have a sexual feeling or feel the need to urinate.

Point 3 - Perineum:

The perineum, the most grounded point as well as the most negative attractive, is between your sexual organs and your anus. The other major grounding point is at the balls of your feet. Your legs have energy channels that connect to the perineum and the channels will bring in more energy without any need to concentrate on the balls of your feet. The upward channel comes from the balls of your feet, over the big toes, up the front of your legs by the shinbones to the kneecaps, and then along the inside of your thighs to join together, connecting at the perineum. The downward energy channel leading from the perineum splits down the back of each of your legs, moves behind the knees, down your calf, and under the heel of your foot, connecting to the balls of your feet. When the perineum window is open, you will feel grounded and be able to handle issues of self easily.

Point 4 - Sacrum:

The sacrum is the flat bone behind your pelvic bone in back and below/between your hips, shaped roughly like a triangle, where many nerve endings come out through four holes on each side. The sacrum is not your tailbone, which is below and connects to it. When the energy window of the sacral pump is open, we feel that our past is working to our benefit. I'm sure you have all met people who continually complain about their past, how they were brought up, neglected, abused, and so forth. Similarly, you have met other people who have had just as much difficulty, and yet they claim that their past experiences are what made them strong and who they are today. These are cases of a closed sacral pump window versus an open one.

Point 5 - Kidneys:

The kidneys are right across from the navel but on either side of the spine in back. In Western medical terms, the kidneys' function is to filter the waste fluids that you then excrete. The kidneys represent the energy of gentleness. When the kidney window is open, you will easily connect and behave with gentleness, and when the window is closed, you will more readily have fear in everyday life.

Point 6 - Adrenal Glands:

The adrenal glands are just above the kidneys and directly across from the solar plexus on either side of the spine. The adrenal glands are the energy distributor cap for your physical body engine as well as the spiritual realm. When the adrenal window is open, you will feel full of energy and ready to take on any project. When closed, you will feel lackluster and have difficulty being enthusiastic.

Point 7 - Spinal Point- Mid-Vertebrae 5/6:

Point 7 is between vertebrae 5 and 6, across from your

heart center, or breastbone, and between your shoulder blades. When this window is open, you will have feelings of forgiveness, freedom, and gratitude toward yourself and others. When closed, you will feel bitter about yourself and others.

Point 8 - Cervical Vertebra 7:

Cervical vertebra 7, or point 8, is the little bump you can feel sticking out on your spine right at the beginning of the neck where your shoulders come together. This window is directly across from your throat point, in the hollow where your clavicle comes together. This window on your spine, when open, will give you the feeling of connection to yourself and to others. People who do not have this window well open often tend to be reclusive and lacking in self- worth, especially when the lower windows along the spine are not well opened.

Point 9 - Cranial-Sacral Pump:

The cranial-sacral pump, point 9, is where the bottom of your skull, identified by a small protrusion of the bone, connects to the top of your neck. By having your head straight, chin tucked in, this window is across from your mid-eyebrow point. The cranial-sacral window controls the energetic breath and is associated with inspiration. When it is open, you will be inspired in all your decisions and projects. By energetic breath I mean the pulse of our spinal fluid, which is important not only to our spiritual energy but also to our physical well-being.

Point 10 - Crown:

The crown, point 10, is associated with the pineal gland deep in the brain. This window is the most positive propulsive. When we sit straight, the crown window is in a direct line above the perineum, or negative attractive, and can be located by moving your fingers straight up from each ear until they connect at the top of your head. Many times you will be able to feel a slight depression or suture point. The crown window and pineal gland are associated with a higher purpose or clear direction for ourselves, both energetically and, if developed, even physically. Birds have the most developed pineal glands, which is what gives them their direction when flying north and south during migration, relocating their previous habitat. The pineal is our compass on all levels.

Point 11 - Pituitary Gland:

Point 11, or the pituitary gland, is deep inside the brain under the pineal gland. This point is often referred to as the third eye. When open, this window gives us a sense of knowing that can be described as intuition or can manifest in clairvoyance or clairaudiance. This window opening is helpful to our ability to align all the parts of ourselves for clear action, enabling us to engage fully.

Point 12 - Tongue:

The tongue, point 12, is only important as a switch connecting the front energy channel to the back energy channel. The tongue should be placed wherever it feels comfortable when we start moving energy.

Point 13 - Throat Center:

The throat center is at the top of the chest at the hollow

of the clavicle/throat connection. The throat window controls our dreams and communication at many levels. This sensitive point should not be overenergized. When it is open, we can both receive and send communications clearly.

Point 14 - Heart:

The heart, point 14, is located over the thymus gland. For men it is found at the midpoint between the nipples, and for women at the mid-breastbone point. This is the window to love, compassion, respect, and joy. When closed in the extreme, this window will produce cruelty and/or hatred either toward self or others. When it is open, we have great joy in our life in the broadest sense.

Point 15 - Solar Plexus:

The solar plexus, point 15 on the diagram, is at the base of our chest, the center line just below the breastbone or rib cage. This window is usually well developed by most business people because it is the window of power and responsibility. When the window is not properly open, business people many times will seek the power without assuming the responsibility connected to the gift.

Closing the Loop - Navel:
From the solar plexus we reconnect down to the navel in order to close the loop.

I have described the points in the sequence of the positive propulsive side of the life force because it is easier to feel and connect to a pushing energy versus a pulling energy. For both, the points or windows are the same and are equally important and must be opened equally in each direction. When the two circuits have been completed, we can enter the quiet, deep space of the neutral point.

Getting Started
To further open to subtler levels, and increase our consciousness during meditation, I recommend sitting in a chair rather than crosslegged in the Indian or Hindu style. I find that this sitting position keeps us more open and connects us better to the negative attractive and

positive propulsive energies of the life force. The planet, or Mother Earth as the Native Americans would say, is the physical embodiment of the negative attractive—the pull. Where would we be without gravity? When we sit erect in a chair we continually ground ourselves through the balls of our feet, the K-1 or kidney-one point in acupuncture terms, sometimes known as the bubbling spring. Think about running barefoot through the grass on a hot summer day—how cooling and grounding that feeling is. Our other major point of grounding is through the perineum, located halfway between our sexual organs and our anus, which is the lowest and most negative attractive point of our torso. Grounding is about being fully present and clear. The more we ground the better we will be able to handle higher life force energies and attract the positive propulsive to match our needs. Think of the function of a lightning rod. It is used to attract the lightning, the most positive propulsive. Once we are well grounded, our crown, which is the top of our head, can be open to receive the positive propulsive, the Father Sky energy referred to by Native Americans. All meditative sitting positions are based on a pyramid with three points on the ground and one point thrusting toward the sky. The Hindu system uses the two knees of the crosslegged position and the perineum as ground with the crown of the head as point. Once you have mastered the basic sitting position in a chair, you may use the crosslegged position if you desire. I sit crosslegged from time to time, but only after I feel that I am properly grounded. Another consideration is that when you have your hands together, the major energy channel running through your palms is connected and therefore the loop is closed.

To begin the meditation, sit in a chair in a meditative position with your back straight, thighs parallel to the ground, both feet on the ground, and tongue at the roof of your mouth, either just behind the teeth or in the middle of the palate or curled back to the soft part of the palate, whichever is most comfortable. Place your hands in your lap, left palm up, right palm down, clasped together. Close your eyes and smile in your eyes. Keep your chin slightly tucked and your shoulders relaxed. Now you are in the proper posture.

The Positive Propulsive Route

Point 1

Focus your attention on your navel. Imagine looking down internally at your navel and feel a slight whirling energy approximately the size of a quarter, or visualize it as light or vibration or warmth. Notice how you experience it. For some people this energy may be experienced either as a vibration, a tingling, warmth, color, light, or even sound. Or it may appear primarily as a kind of inner knowing. Initially you may even believe it is a figment of your imagination. Accept and allow whatever way your body-mind chooses to manifest it to you—everyone is individual. Become conscious of the energy window at your navel.

Point 2

Now bring your attention down to your sexual center. Look down inwardly with your eyes to your sexual energy window, while still feeling energy at the navel. Feel, see, experience the quarter-size energy whirling there and then, on an exhale, imagine that you are pushing the energy down from your navel window using your eyes internally to connect to your sexual window. Relax and do this without straining as you move the energy down. Let your breath push the energy down.

Point 3

Bring your consciousness down to your perineum. Feel the energy whirl at that window. On an exhale, push the energy down from your sexual center to your perineum. Always use your eyes internally to help the process. Be aware of your energy connection from your navel to your sexual center and then perineum.

Point 4

Next is the sacral window. Feel the energy whirling and look internally at your sacrum. On an inhale, push the energy up and connect to your sacrum. If you concentrate you will notice that your sacrum can move forward and back slightly, maybe an eighth of an inch, independently from your pelvis. This slight movement can function as a pump to move the energy up your spine or forward toward your perineum. To feel the connection better you can move your sacrum one-eighth to a quarter of an inch backward and forward while you sit. Sometimes the energy will feel as if it is spiraling around the sacrum; this is quite normal.

Point 5

Now bring your attention to your kidney window. Feel the concentrated energy whirl on your spine. On an inhale, use your sacral pump by pushing the energy up the spine and connect your sacrum to your kidney point.

Point 6

Bring your energy focus and your eyes to your adrenal point. On an inhale, push the energy connection from the kidney point to the adrenal window. Again, you may want to use the sacral pump to facilitate the movement. Feel the energy. Be aware that you now have an energy connection from navel to sexual center, perineum, sacrum, kidney, and now adrenal windows.

Point 7

Next, bring your focus to thorax vertebrae 5 and 6 on the diagram, and feel the energy point develop. Inhale, pushing upward the energy connection from adrenal point to thorax 5/6. The sacrum can be used to help move the energy all the way up. Take as much time as you need to feel the connection. The points that appear more difficult will indicate some sort of blockage or resistance—be patient with yourself. Again, you may even think that what you feel is a figment of your imagination. Stay with it. Eventually the energy movement will be natural and quite quick.

Point 8

Place your attention at cervical vertebra 7, that bump at the back of the neck where the shoulders meet, and look energetically backward to that window and energize it. Sense the energy whirling. Inhale up, pushing the connection from thorax 5/6.

Point 9

Next, bring your consciousness to the cranial-sacral

pump point at the bottom of your skull/neck connection. Look backward to the point and inhale the energy up, pushing from cervical 7 to the cranial-sacrum window. This energy pump can be activated by clenching and releasing the teeth and jaw, but such physical movement is only necessary when you feel that the energy is not moving. This is where all the major nerves enter your spine to be distributed throughout your body. It is a crucial and difficult point to feel at times.

Point 10

At the crown point, focus your eyes upward and inhale up, remembering that the cranial-sacrum point is also a pump. You can clench and release your jaw to help the energy through the tight connection of cranium and neck. On the other hand, you may experience the energy exploding into your cranium and see various colors and even star points of light. If this happens, concentrate the energy, using your consciousness and your eye focus to bring it to the crown point. Feel the positive propulsive connection coming in through your crown window.

Point 11

Now bring your attention to the mid-eyebrow window and, exhaling, push down, connecting into the energy from the crown window to the mid-eyebrow. Again, you may experience light or color movement. At each point you intend to connect the energy, first energize it with your focus of a quarter-size energy whirl. Remember you are now connected from your navel all the way around to your mid-eyebrow window.

Point 12

Next, deliver the energy through the tongue "switch" down to the throat point. You may want to move your tongue around on your palate to feel energetically the clearest or most subtle connection. You may also find that the energy coming down from your mid-eyebrow follows the ridge of your nose or splits on either side, then moves through your tongue and travels down your throat to the throat window.

Point 13

First convey your focus of energy to the throat center and

then make the connection on an exhale, pushing down from mid-eyebrow through the tongue. Do not spend a long time on the throat center, since it is very sensitive.

Point 14

Now bring your consciousness to the heart center. Energize your heart center and then connect the energy to your throat point, exhaling to push it down to your heart window. You may feel warmth and an expansion in your chest. Tears of joy may come to your eyes; this is quite normal.

Point 15

The last point is the solar plexus window. Energize it as you did the others and connect from the heart point.

Closing the Loop

Finally, reconnect to point 1, the navel, which closes the loop. Pause there for a moment. You may notice that your hands get warm; that is because the energy also travels down your arms within the loop of your clasped hands.

Now we must do the same loop in reverse to complete the negative attractive route and be in balance to go into our deeper meditative space of the neutral force.

The Negative Attractive Route

A. Start at the navel, point 1, but instead of pushing down, focus and activate the solar plexus, point 15, and pull up. Similar to the positive propulsive cycle, you will feel or imagine a quarter-size energy at the center activating it before pulling from the previous point.

B. From the solar plexus, inhale the energy, pulling up from the navel. The pulling action has a very different feel and is more subtle, so you really need to pay attention with your full focus.

C. Next, activate your heart center, point 14, and pull the energy from the solar plexus.

D. Continue around the circle, this time pulling from the new window the energy from the previous window instead of pushing the old to the new. Using the diagram pull from point 13 then 12 all the way back to point 1, the navel. Do this using your consciousness and your eyes traveling in reverse, up the front and down the back, until you have reconnected to the navel.

When you are complete and reconnected to your navel, stop and concentrate the energy. Some practices will give you elaborate counting exercises to do this. However, I found that by simply focusing your intent of pulling all your energy down into an *ever-decreasing spiral* at the navel, you will bring the energy to a point. For women, spiral down the energy counterclockwise, starting around the navel with the size of a half dollar and cranking it down to the size of a grain of sand. For men, do the exact same thing but clockwise. This grain of sand is the storage of the increased life force, which in Taoist and Buddhist practices is referred to as your pearl.

For me, particularly when I first started, I felt as if the positive propulsive side was like pushing thick syrup from one point to the next. Some windows were particularly difficult, and I felt great heat develop (I will explore this point further in the next chapter). The negative attractive, the pulling, felt much easier from the start, like a cool breeze or a light, flowing movement. I soon discovered that I could bring my attention, and eyes, to my crown and pull in one fell swoop up from the navel, feeling the energy as a ribbon traveling up to my crown. Then I would focus on my perineum and pull the energy from the crown, feeling the energy as a thin, light waterfall. And finally, I would pull back up to the navel. I would suggest only using this procedure when you are sure the intermediate windows are fully open. Although this circulation may be subtler, it will also be easier because the male pushing, which is more readily felt, will have already partially opened the route.

I recommend you do the positive propulsive and the negative attractive cycles at least three times and preferably in multiples of nine, then concentrate the energy when both male and female cycles are totally complete. You will find that once you are accustomed to the practice, the energy will flow around in a matter of seconds. Do not forget to use your eyes. Know that this source of the life force connection, the pearl, will always be available to you and the more you practice the stronger it will grow. Anytime you are faced with a decision, you can connect to the source and quickly develop full intent.

The Neutral Force

A. Give thanks to your mind for helping you through the energy circulation and ask it to be quiet and receive during the rest of the practice. You are still sitting in a meditative position. After you become familiar with the practice, you may find that ten minutes or less have elapsed. If you want, extend the circulation time. Sometimes, in this quiet mode, the energy may circulate on its own.

B. When you have finished, sit quietly, let your mind go blank, and allow yourself to receive a deeper knowing or clarity about business actions or personal issues. This quiet time is extremely important and can last three minutes or three hours—it's up to you. In the beginning you may find yourself fidgety because of the distractions of your day's schedule.

C. Start by allocating fifteen to twenty minutes and set an alarm, if you have a time constraint, to make sure you come back to the reality of the business world. You may find you can only handle five minutes, however, and that's fine. Allow your own internal clock to determine the duration. If your consciousness and whole being are expanding tremendously, then allocate more time. You are in charge and must decide your priorities.

D. Several possibilities might develop. You may experience a flood of new ideas and creative concepts. I find that keeping a notepad and pen handy is helpful in recording any information since I cannot always remember the entire sequence of the communication. However, after writing, it may be difficult to reconnect to that deep space of the neutral force in mind and body. You will need to experiment to see whether you can remember enough information by staying in the neutral point rather than breaking that special meditative space to record the input. I find that most times the decision for a particular direction is made *for* me and I allow either just remaining in meditation or recording the insight. Each meditation is different.

E. Furthermore, instead of ideas, thoughts, or concepts coming forward, you might find yourself in an extremely deep space, developing a profound knowing that cannot be expressed in words. This experience might manifest in the form of colors and/or warm currents of energy. This deep knowing might also appear as a heart opening, and this usually occurs with tears of joy streaming down your cheeks. Sometimes this will even start in the active part of the meditation before you have reached the neutral point.

F. One last point regarding the meditation. When you decide you are complete, open your eyes very slowly, a slit at a time, to let light in and reconnect to the present. Try to do this even if you have set an alarm and it has startled you in your meditation. After your eyes are fully open, rub your hands together and brush them down your forehead, cheeks, throat, and chest as if you are brushing down dust or energy, to help yourself be fully grounded.

When you have memorized the points and the route, and have clearly felt the energy move, you can eliminate using inhales and exhales for energy movement. These are only helpful guides when you start the meditation. You will find that as the meditation becomes more familiar, you will guide less and less with your mind and will feel the life force going where it needs to go. Also, the quiet time will become easier and more profound.

In Summary

1. The more we work with the life force connection meditation, the greater the flow, and the more in tune we will be while developing greater clarity, intuition, and inner guidance in our business decisions and our life. The more we allow the life force to flow, the more we will be

certain of our true purpose and be able to develop full intent for right action.

2. The life force connection meditation is the foundation of spirituality for our business actions. It deals with us as individuals in our relation to the life force, the current from Universal Knowledge.

Although I have focused on the business applications for this practice in previous chapters, I would like to emphasize that the practice has its greatest importance when it is interwoven into all aspects of life. We all have the life force flowing through us, otherwise we would not be alive. The question is how free or constricted it is and how it affects our lives. The more open the flow, the less inhibited we are and the more we are in touch with our self. Ultimately, it connects to the greatest computer of all, Universal Knowledge. I hope you will find the life force connection meditation useful. Good luck and have great joy in your practice.

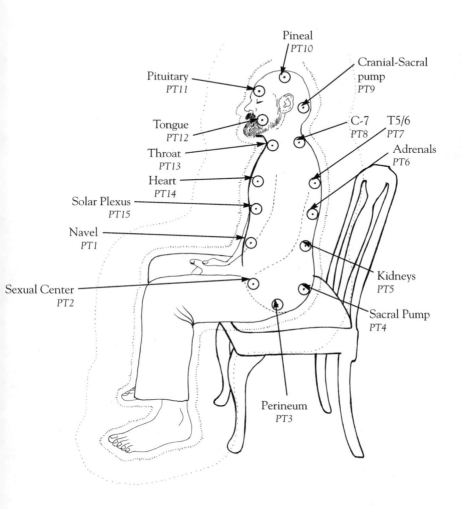

Pineal
PT10

Cranial-Sacral
pump
PT9

Pituitary
PT11

Tongue
PT12

C-7
PT8

T5/6
PT7

Adrenals
PT6

Throat
PT13

Heart
PT14

Solar Plexus
PT15

Navel
PT1

Sexual Center
PT2

Kidneys
PT5

Sacral Pump
PT4

Perineum
PT3

CHAPTER 6

STAYING ON THE PATH

The side effects may prove challenging

By September 1984, my company was incurring major losses due to legal and reexport costs on coffees purchased from an unreliable source. I had sold my company effective the end of 1984, so it was important to finish the year financially strong because of pending agreements. At this time I was committed to the life force connection meditation, which I practiced faithfully. On average, I usually spent ten minutes of active energy movement through the channels, then twenty to thirty minutes in the place of the deep neutral force. One time, during a moment in the neutral point, I had a revelation about how to resolve our financial impasse.

As I was in this quiet space, I kept receiving pictures of a large harbor in Africa with many ships anchored at its entrance or at the docks. I continued to exhale deeper to remain in this special space, trying to keep monkey mind out. The image revealed a familiar part of West Africa, but the scene was abnormally quiet. I could not understand the communication, and finally monkey mind came in, urging me to go to the office.

On the drive to New York I returned to the images often. When I arrived at the office I inquired of the traders if anything was going on in West Africa. Within an hour we received confirmation that the port of Abidjan in the Ivory Coast had labor problems and was totally shut down. The Ivory Coast was the largest shipping country of robusta coffees and, therefore, the closing of its port would influence the London futures market (see Appendix B for trading definitions). London futures had been trading down in a bear market with many shorts outstanding. After a major meeting of our traders, with full intent we decided to buy the futures market and go long. This could put a squeeze on the market due to a lack of supplies. While we became aggressive buyers, the futures market slowly turned up, enhancing the value of our physical coffees in the process. In the aforementioned incident, the *do-re-mi* of the octave was operating well.

Suddenly, a large Singapore trading house became major sellers against us. The first threshold guardian of resistance had been encountered. During a morning meditation, I felt strongly that we needed to stay with our decision to buy coffees but also sensed an urgency for outside assistance. We redoubled our efforts and put out the word through a trusted informant in Singapore that we were intending to take delivery of the London January futures position. The Singapore trading house took heed, turned their position around, and became important buyers as well. The resistance had been surmounted and we were in full stride in the *fa-so-la-ti* part of the octave. The market was going straight up, and by the end of December our financials were in excellent shape. As 1985 began, we found ourselves in the gap between octaves, a timely position to conclude the sale of the company. The significant part of this story for me involved the clear communication I received from Universal Knowledge in the meditation. Before I could come to this deep trust of the communication I had received, I had worked through a lot of experiences. Let us review these point-by-point:

1. At first, some people are not sure that the life force is really flowing because it can be subtle, or they may be convinced that what they feel is a figment of their imagination. Stay with it; the energy flow may at first seem minuscule, but in time all your points or windows will open. In unusual cases the flow might be fully open in six months with consistent practice. In other instances it might take five years. This is not a competition. Each person is different and needs to develop at his or her own pace.

2. The important part is not achieving immediate openings but rather the discovery of self and the increased consciousness that develops in the decision-making process. I found that meditations would vary between offering me greater insights into my business, as in the aforementioned story, and raising questions about blockages and resistances. I found that in either case I became more effective as a business person.

3. The path to greater consciousness and clarity in

business actions and in life is difficult. Reading this book or taking one seminar will not develop your ultimate consciousness or make you enlightened. You will need to work at it, and the road is strewn with potholes. It is important to develop your full intent to complete the first *do-re-mi*. And then, encountering the first resistance in the octave, the first threshold guardian, you will have to redouble your efforts to reach the *fa-so-la-ti* part of the octave. But be assured, if you start with full intent and a deep urge, the life force will support you.

4. Enlightenment does not exist by itself except when you have reconnected to Universal Knowledge. If you reach an epiphany in feeling, color, light, or emotions, any particular one or the entire range of these together, enjoy this to the fullest. This experience usually signifies the attainment and completion of the first octave and the life force taking you through the gap to the next octave. Do not fall in love with this space however, but renew your deep intent to achieve the *do-re-mi* of the next octave. This will be ongoing until you reconnect to the ultimate source.

A discussion of possible experiences you may have in meeting threshold guardians follows.

1. Most people report the generation of considerable heat when first starting the life force connection meditation practice. I actually used to become so warm that I would take off my clothes, layer by layer, and end up meditating in my underwear even though the room was cool. This is quite normal, as our bodies are not used to handling increased energy at first. An analogy to this experience might be current going through a wire that is too small to handle the electricity and, therefore, generates heat. After a period of time the body adjusts and the resistances or blockages open, a larger channel develops, the heat disappears.

2. You will notice the heat or ache principally where you have the greatest stress as the energy attempts to flow through the constrictions. In my case, as for many men, I carried my stress in my upper back and neck, armored as I was to go forth to meet the world. As this physical manifestation appeared, the related emotional and mental issues of my life presented themselves to me in the quiet neutral

force portion of the meditation. In other words, the patterns and attitudes that no longer are working for us will come to mind through Universal Knowledge communication. The physical constrictions are the manifestations of our bad patterns and attitudes. Later, as I progressed in the meditations and my upper back became open, I found the resistance in my neck. It became so stiff that I felt as if an iron rod had been jammed down the back of my skull through my spine. This also passed in time.

3. The road is not easy, and just when you are about to quit because it is a lot of work, a tremendous, joyful revelation comes to you in the neutral point. The joyful feeling is so great that you continue the practice in the hope of duplicating it. The outcome of each meditation is different and no preconceived results will manifest, so enjoy the surprises.

4. Other practitioners have reported an ache or stress in their lower backs. However, make sure this is not just mechanical. You may need another cushion to raise your buttocks and be more comfortable. Still others have developed diarrhea for up to two days as energy cleansed

the abdomen. Some people have reported fluttering in their stomach muscles or fascia, while others shake throughout their bodies. Over time, all these phenomena settle down as your body adjusts to the increased flow of energy. It is always a good idea for you to check with your health-care practitioner if you think there is a physical issue not related to the practice.

5. One precaution involves headaches or chest pains, especially for people with high blood pressure or heart issues. If these are present, bring the energy flow down immediately to your navel, which is the balance point. If you still feel aches or heat in the upper areas, bring the energy down to your perineum and split it down the inside back of your legs to the balls of your feet and totally ground the energy into the earth. If you have any physical issues, you should work with a health-care practitioner. And as a safety precaution, stop this meditation practice until the problem is resolved. Remember, you are in charge and must take responsibility for your decisions.

6. When first starting the practice, some people find they cannot connect or move energy through their cra-

nial-sacral point. In this case, short-circuit the head and go right to the throat center or reverse the flow and see if you can connect through the negative attractive side. Do not get upset; eventually you will be able to connect all the points. This may also indicate a blockage and perhaps the need for a chiropractor who is good with neck adjustments, which will help release the physical blockage. A chiropractor who does cranial-sacral work would be beneficial, because the connection of our head to our neck/spine all the way down to our sacrum is crucial to energy flow. Our cranial-spinal fluid has a pulse much as our blood pumping has a pulse. This spinal fluid pulse is in harmony with our breathing and our entire energy nervous system. On a physical plane, proper alignment by a chiropractor helps our connection to the life force on the more subtle levels.

Experiences in the Advanced Practice of Self-Realization

1. Once you have mastered the practice and perform it on a regular basis, you may at times find that your eyelids

open very slightly, a mere slit, letting in light, particularly when connecting to a deeper self during the neutral point of the meditation. This is quite normal, so do not become frustrated and insist on closing your eyes. This just indicates you have reached a deep space, so let it happen naturally. When we have our eyes open we have "out-sight". When we have our eyes closed, we have insight. In Zen Buddhism, one sits with the eyes open only a slit to let in light to symbolize being present with all our senses and at the same time being deeply connected to the more subtle realms. The slit of light coming into the eye denotes the neutral point, not out-sight or insight. Let it happen naturally, as your body and consciousness determine what you need.

2. As you advance in your consciousness and spirituality, other manifestations will occur indicating a greater, and in a way a more subtle, flow of the life force. You may find over time, usually years, that you feel a light tingling sensation along your spine at various times during the day; this indicates a free flow of the life force. However, the most common is the sensation of ants crawling around in

your throat, a tingling I only started experiencing in the last five years. The sensation is much like having a post-nasal drip but without a cold. If you are sure you do not have a cold, stay with the energy sensation. Do not cough or swallow, as this will interrupt the flow, which you want to encourage. You will have to experiment by holding your breath or breathing very slowly. I found that the best action is to open my throat as if to burp, but do not, and let the life force move. It will usually move up and explode into an exquisite sensation in your head. If at first your channels are not fully open, the life force may travel through one eye on the way to the head and give you the same sensation, momentarily, as the coldness of eating ice cream. What is most interesting is that the energy, when it occurs spontaneously, always seems to move in the negative attractive pathway, the energy of receiving.

3. Other phenomena may appear, such as hearing voices or receiving communications, having a vision, or perceiving a particular feeling. These can be either strong or subtle at a deep level; stay tuned and decide how what you receive makes sense for you.

Although these side effects may seem odd, to me they are very exciting because they indicate movement, growth and connection to the life force. I view these effects much like the process of making a fine Japanese sword. The steel must be tempered, hammered and sharpened to become a fine, beautiful weapon. The analogy to the sword represents your true self manifesting into pure clarity and consciousness that can be applied to business.

CHAPTER 7

IN SUMMATION

In a brief and concentrated span, I have tried to introduce you to the spiritual concepts and practices that are applicable to business and that have been refined and translated from twenty years of search and experience. Allow yourself to digest this intense spiritual meal within your own rhythm and time sequence. There is no rush. Go back to the various practices, try them at different times of day and night, and feel them, allowing your knowledge to develop internally down to the molecular level. Trust yourself: trust what you feel, trust the messages you receive, trust that you can always take the appropriate action in business as well as in your personal life. It is important to realize that these practices do not represent a linear progression; rather, one practice enhances another in an ongoing circular manner. As you come to understand and develop the later practices, you can return and deepen the comprehension of earlier practices. Once you develop full intent, then assume responsibility for the consequences of commitment to a particular course of action, without regrets.

A Brief Review

1. We started by getting in touch with ourselves, heightening our awareness through breathing and the smile down meditation. As our awareness developed, we connected to the need to follow our deep urges, desires, and joy, which do not come from the mind but are communicated deep from within our body, from the belly brain. Listen to the communication from Universal Knowledge through your body. Trust the communication, align yourself with it, and behave in your business accordingly.

2. We next explored the concept of full intent and how to activate this principle. The key is to bring our false ego to consciousness so we can realize cooperation between false and true ego. We need to move away from hiding behind our false ego as a representation of self.

Rather, consciously looking at the false ego allows true ego to work with integrity and clarity of purpose on any project. Another benefit resides in the greater internal harmony for personal and business life, while externally, others sense trustworthiness in what you stand for.

3. The Law of Octaves represents the harmonics of how energy movement works in our business world. Nothing ever stands still, the universe is in continual change, and certainly the business world reflects this axiom. The musical scale provides the metaphor for the Law of Octaves. Key concepts involve acknowledging resistances as signals to connect with self before moving forward or redefining the next step. A critical moment occurs at the gap, for here the outcome is beyond our control and we need to entrust the outcome to the life force, the intelligent current of the universe, before moving to the next octave.

4. As mentioned above, we need to access the life force, the intelligent current of Universal Knowledge, in order to ask for help at important junctures of business activity and decision. The conflictive meditation is the vehicle used to

accomplish this. We learn that to do a successful conflictive meditation we have to develop full intent and be fully who we are in the opposing aspects of the life force—that is, the negative attractive and the positive propulsive. When we can connect with deep feeling to the feminine and masculine aspects of the life force, then the neutral force is created by the pull of the opposite aspects to provide closure for a successful business realization.

5. Once we have these tools for our business involvement and our personal lives, we can work with the deepening of our consciousness by doing a life force connection meditation. This meditation facilitates an increase in energies and brings greater clarity, but it also will indicate where any blockages occur in the physical, emotional, and mental realms. Once we have clearly located the various points in the life force connection meditation and the direction of the energy movement, we will be able to do the active part of the meditation in minutes. Upon achieving the neutral point, the resulting quiet time becomes an elective period, whether five minutes or several hours.

The importance of this meditation is that it will raise your consciousness, permitting active participation in other practices, with greater connection. In other words, the life force connection meditation provides the groundwork to enhance awareness, increase the development of full intent, clarify the location within the octave, and realize the aspects of the negative attractive and positive propulsive before unifying toward the neutral point.

With these tools you are well on the way to being a more conscious, spiritual person in your business life. You are in charge and responsible for anything that resonates or does not resonate for you, and you are the one who must decide what you will accept and use or discard. My job is to bring these concepts and practices to your attention as clearly and succinctly as possible. They have worked for me; you will make your own decision. The more we know about ourselves and our consciousness at all levels, the more clearly we can make decisions in business, for our personal lives, and in harmony with all our relations. I use "all our relations" here in the Native American sense, meaning everything—people, animals, insects, trees, vegetation, rocks, Mother Earth, and Father Sky.

Success in any business involvement is a function of connection— connection to self and connection to Universal Knowledge. The deeper the connection, the greater will be your joy. Full intent needs to be engaged to have great joy in any business undertaking. Use the practices you have learned and do not be afraid to bring out the true self, engaging the false ego to experience exhilaration in your business. Be aware that lack of good feeling may mean that the false ego has the upper hand and you need to reevaluate your business involvement. In the final analysis, money and the bottom line mean nothing if you don't experience joy in the process.

> *Love is the virtue of the Heart*
> *Sincerity is the virtue of the Mind*
> *Courage is the virtue of the Spirit*
> *Decision is the virtue of the Will*
>
> —Frank Lloyd Wright

Appendix A

The Life Force Connection Meditation
Quick Reference Guide

A. Positive Propulsive—Energize:

Point 1: Navel

Point 2: Sexual center—push energy down from navel

Point 3: Perineum—push energy down from navel

Point 4: Sacrum—push energy up from perineum

Point 5: Kidneys—push energy up from sacrum

Point 6: Adrenal glands—push energy up from kidneys

Point 7: Thorax vertabrae 5/6—push energy up from adrenals

Point 8: Cervical vertabra 7—push energy up from thorax

Point 9: Cranial-sacral—push energy up from cervical

Point 10: Crown (pineal)—push energy up from cranial-sacral

Point 11: Third eye (pituitary)—push energy down from crown

Point 12: Tongue—do not energize, but push energy through tongue, placed at roof of the mouth, to throat center

Point 13: Throat—push down from third eye.

Point 14: Heart—push down from throat

Point 15: Solar plexus—push down from heart

Close: Navel—push down from solar plexus

B.   Negative Attractive—Energize:

Point 1:   Navel

Point 15: Solar plexus—pull up from navel

Point 14: Heart—pull up from solar plexus

Point 13: Throat—pull up from heart

Point 12: Tongue—feel energy pull through it

Point 11: Third eye (pituitary)—pull up from throat

Point 10: Crown (pineal)—pull up from third eye

Point 9:   Cranial-sacral—pull down from crown

Point 8:   Vertebra cervical 7—pull down from
           cranial-sacral

Point 7:   Vertebrae thorax 5/6—pull down from
           cervical 7

Point 6:   Adrenals—pull down from thorax 5/6

Point 5:   Kidneys—pull down from adrenals

Point 4:   Sacrum—pull down from kidneys

Point 3:   Perenium—pull down from sacrum

Point 2:   Sexual center— pull up from perenium

Close: Navel—pull up from sexual center

Concentrate energy in an ever-decreasing circle into a pearl—women circling counterclockwise; men clockwise. Start the period of quiet time, connecting to the neutral force. At the finish of quiet time, open your eyes slowly and brush energy down cheeks, throat, and chest.

Appendix B

The following definitions are for those unfamiliar with commodity trading:

Futures Market: A place where a commodity such as coffee is bought for future acceptance or sold for future delivery (in terms of months).

Note: In most cases, traders on futures markets do not accept or deliver the physical commodity but rather settle the difference between the market price and their contract price in currency (dollars, pounds, etc. . . .).

Long: The position of owning a commodity (coffee) with the intent of reselling it at a higher price.

Short: The position of selling a commodity (coffee) that the seller does not possess with the intent of purchasing it at a lower price.

Taking Delivery: The act of taking physical delivery of a commodity (coffee) from a futures market.

Note: This action usually causes a pressure on any short positions that do not own the physical commodity (coffee) to deliver and forces them to pay increasingly higher prices to get out of their contract.

BIBLIOGRAPHY

The books that follow influenced both my business and spiritual development. I've included books that came before my spiritual involvement that I felt were important because of the energy they imparted to my consciousness at the time. Many of these books will enable the readers to further deepen their knowledge on particular subjects discussed or hinted at in this book.

Buddhism

Fremantle, Francesca, and Ch^gyam Trungpa. *The Tibetan Book of the Dead.* Boulder, CO: Shambala Publications, Inc., 1975.

Govinda, Luma Anagarika. *Foundations of Tibetan Mysticism.* York Beach, ME: Samuel Weiser, Inc., 1969.

Gyaltsen, Khenpo Rimpoche. *The Garland of Mohamudra Practices.* Ed. by Katherine Rogers. Ithaca, NY: Snow Lion Publications, 1986.

Kapleau, Philip. *The Three Pillars of Zen.* New York: Anchor Press/Doubleday, 1980.

Nanh, Thich Nhat. *The Miracle of Mindfulness.* Boston: Beacon

Press, 1975.

Reps, Paul. *Zen Flesh, Zen Bones*. Garden City, NY: Anchor Books, orig. 1930.

Snying-Po, Nam-mkha'i. *Mother of Knowledge*. Trans. by Tarthang Tulku. Berkeley, CA: Dharma Publishing, 1983.

Suzuki, Shunryu. *Zen Mind, Beginner's Mind*. Tokyo, Japan: John Wootherhill, Inc., 1970.

Thien-An, Thich. *Zen Philosophy, Zen Practice*. Berkeley, CA: Dharma Publishing, 1975.

Tsogyal, Yeshe. *The Lotus-Born*. Revealed by Ral Nyiamaser. Boston, MA: Shambala Publications, Inc., 1993.

Business

Drucker, Peter F. *The Age of Discontinuity*. New York: Harper & Row, 1968.

Drucker, Peter F. *Managing in Turbulent Times*. New York: Harper & Row, 1980.

Jaworski, Joseph. *Synchronicity*. San Francisco, CA: Berrett-Kohler Publishers, Inc., 1996

Josephson, Matthew. *The Robber Barons*. New York: Harcourt Brace, 1934.

Musashi, Miyamoto. *A Book of Five Rings*. Trans. by Victor Harris. Woodstock, NY: The Overlook Press, 1974.

Peters, Thomas L., and Robert W. Waterman, Jr. *In Search of Excellence*. New York: Harper & Row, 1982.

Toffler, Alvin. *The Third Wave*. New York: William Morrow &

Company, 1980.

Tzu, Sun. *The Art of War*. Trans. by Thomas Cleary. Boston, MA: Shambala Publications, Inc., 1988.

Consciousness-General

Campbell, Joseph, and Bill Moyers. *The Power of Myth*. Ed. by Betty Sue Flowers. New York: Doubleday, 1988.

Chopra, Deepak. *The Seven Spiritual Laws of Success*. San Rafael, CA: Amber-Allen Publishing and New World Library, 1994.

Monroe, Robert A. *Far Journeys*. New York: Bantam Doubleday Dell Publishing, 1984.

Monroe, Robert A. *Journeys Out of the Body*. New York: Doubleday & Company, 1971.

Pirsig, Robert M. *Zen and the Art of Motorcycle Maintenance*. New York: William Morrow & Company, 1974.

Shah, Indries. *The Way of the Sufi*. London: Arkana, 1968.

Tompkins, Peter, and Christopher Bird. *The Secret Life of Plants*. New York: Harper & Row, 1972.

Eastern Mysticism/Wisdom/Christianity

de Chardin, Teilhard Pierre. *The Divine Milieu*. New York: Harper & Row, 1960.

de Chardin, Teilhard Pierre. *The Future of Man*. New York: Harper & Row, 1964.

Fox, Matthew. *The Coming of the Cosmic Christ*. San Francisco: Harper & Row, 1988.

Fox, Matthew. *Original Blessings*. Santa Fe, NM: Bear & Company, 1983.

Gurdjieff, G.I. *Meetings with Remarkable Men*. New York: Dutton, 1974.

Hatengdi, M.V. *Nityananda*. Cambridge, MA: Rudra Press, 1984.

Mann, John. *Rudi*. Cambridge, MA: Rudra Press, 1987.

Mann, John, and Larr Short. *The Body of Light*. New York: Globe Press Books, 1990.

Radha, Swami Sivananda. *Kundalini Yoga for the West*. Boston, MA: Shambala Publications, Inc., 1978.

Rudi, Swami Rudrananda. *Spiritual Cannibalism*. Woodstock, NY: The Overlook Press, 1978.

Rudi, Swami Rudrananda. *Behind the Cosmic Curtain*. Ed. by John Mann. Arlington, MA: Neolog Publishing, 1984.

West, John Anthony. *Serpent in the Sky*. New York: The Julien Press, 1987, 1979.

General

Bach, Richard. *Illusions: The Adventures of a Reluctant Messiah*. New York: Dell Books, 1977.

Benson, Herbert. *The Relaxation Response*. New York: Avon Books, 1975.

Johnson, Robert A. *Ecstasy*. San Francisco: Harper San Francisco, 1987.

Johnson, Robert A. *Owning Your Own Shadow*. San Francisco: Harper San Francisco, 1991.

Lawler, Robert. *Voices of the First Day*. Rochester, VT: Inner Traditions, 1991.

Millman, Don. *The Way of the Peaceful Warrior*. Tiburon, CA: H.J. Kramer, Inc., 1984.

Myer, Friedman, and Roy H. Rosemon. *Type A Behavior and Your Heart*. New York: Faucett Book Group, 1982.

Upledger, John, with Don Cohen. *An Introduction to Cranial-Sacral Therapies*. Berkeley, CA: North Atlantic Books, 1996.

Vogler, Christopher. *The Writer's Journey*. Studio City, CA: Michael Wiese Productions, 1992.

Physics

Capra, Fritjof. *The Tao of Physics*. Boston, MA: Shambala Publications, 1975.

Hawking, Stephen W. *A Brief History of Time*. New York: Bantam Books, 1988.

Heisenberg, Werner. *Philosophy and Problems of Quantum Physics*. Woodbridge, CT: Oxbow Press, 1952.

Taoism

Chia, Mantak. *Awaken Healing Energy Through the Tao*. New York: Aurora Press, 1983.

Chia, Mantak, and Maniwan Chia. *Fusion of the Five Elements I*. Huntington, NY: Healing Tao Books, 1989

Hoff, Benjamin. *The Tao of Pooh*. New York: Penguin Books, 1983.

Hua Ching, Ni. *The Gentle Path of Spiritual Progress.* Malibu, CA: The Shrine of the Eternal Breath of Tao, 1987.

Tzu, Lao. *Tao Te Ching.* Trans. by Gia-Fu Feng and Jane English. New York: Viking Press, 1972.

Claude Saks is available for lectures and workshops.
Please contact:
Heartsfire Books
500 N. Guadalupe Street, Suite G-465
Santa Fe, New Mexico 87501 USA.
(505) 820-8446
Email: heartsfirebooks@heartsfirebooks.com
Visit us at http://www.heartsfirebooks.com

 ℋEARTSFIRE ℬOOKS

Heartsfire celebrates spiritual evolution in the contemporary world with books that inspire growth and promote physical and spiritual healing. We are privileged to present original and compelling writers who speak from their hearts and guide us to the magic of everyday experience. If you have a manuscript that you feel is suitable for us, we would love to hear from you. Send a letter of inquiry to: *Acquisitions Editor*, **Heartsfire Books**, 500 N. Guadalupe Street, Suite G-465, Santa Fe, New Mexico 87501 USA. Email: heartsfirebooks@heartsfirebooks.com

Heartsfire Spirituality Series

Message from the Sparrows:
Engaging Consciousness
Taylor Morris

The Emerald Covenant:
Spiritual Rites of Passage
Michael E. Morgan

Inescapable Journey:
A Spiritual Adventure
Claude Saks

The Alchemy of Love:
A Pilgrimage of Sacred Discovery
Robert Boldman

Hermanos de la Luz:
Brothers of the Light
Ray John de Aragón

Tibet:
Enduring Spirit, Exploited Land
Robert Z. Apte and Andrés R. Edwards
Foreword and Poem by His Holiness the Dalai Lama

Gifts from Spirit:
A Skeptic's Path
Dennis Augustine

Strong Brew:
One Man's Prelude to Change
Claude Saks

The Search for David:
A Cosmic Journey of Love
George Schwimmer

In the Presence of My Enemies:
Memoirs of Tibetan Nobleman
Tsipon Shuguba
Sumner Carnahan with Lama Kunga Rinpoche

Spirtuality for the Business Person:
Inner Practices for Success
Claude Saks
September 1998

Heartsfire Healing Series

Healing Depression:
A Guide to Making Intelligent
Choices about Treating Depression
Catherine Carrigan

Fathers:
Transforming Your Relationship
John Selby

Health for Life:
Secrets of Tibetan Ayurveda
Robert Sachs
Foreword by Dr. Lobsang Rapgay

Solitude:
The Art of Being with Yourself
John Selby
October 1998